Gifts of
the Spirit

by
Charles McGregor

Gifts of the Spirit
ISBN 0-88144-413-8
Copyright © 2009 by Charles McGregor

Published by
Victory Publishing
A division of
Yorkshire Publishing Group
9731 East 54th Street
Tulsa, OK 74146
www.yorkshirepublishing.com

Foreword

As I travel around the world for the last 30 years being in over 3,000 churches there is one thing that I have notice. There is little understanding of the Gifts of the Spirit in the Local Church. The Holy spirit desires to move among us but needs to use us to do it. Many Christians are not aware of his leading because don't they have an understanding of the gifts of the Spirit. Pastor Charles McGregor a dear close friend of mine has written a very practical and profound teaching on the Gifts of the Spirit. If you have a desire to be used of God in these last days this is a must read.

A Pastor's Friend,
Dr. Buddy Bell
bb@mohi.org
www.BuddyBellMinistries.com
www.SayItBetterLive.com—Live Broadcasting

Contents

1

We Need the Fullness of God

From reading First Corinthians 12, the teaching on the nine gifts of the Spirit, we see that the Apostle Paul wanted Christians to understand our need for the fullness of God. We need everything that God has for us. We need to be equipped with the power of God for our own lives and for ministry.

There have been tough times and there will be more tough times, but how many of us realize that when we operate in these nine gifts of the Spirit that Paul is talking about in this passage, we don't have to fear tomorrow. We don't have to fear what the president and congress are going to do or aren't going to do, or what the economy looks like, or anything else.

Before we look at First Corinthians 12 in detail, I want to cover a few basic points. Everybody needs to be filled with the Spirit of God. Every man, woman, boy, and girl need to be filled with the Spirit. Romans 8:26 tells us the Spirit makes intercession for us. *Likewise the Spirit also helpeth our infirmities: for we know not what we should pray for as we ought: but the Spirit itself maketh intercession for us with groanings which cannot be uttered.* However, there are some doctrines taught having to do with being filled with the Spirit that just don't line up with the Bible.

There is a teaching that a person may be filled with the Holy Ghost without ever speaking in tongues. The problem with this doctrine is that it just isn't supported by the Bible. All the people we read about in the Bible who were filled with the Spirit spoke in tongues as the Spirit gave them utterance. Speaking in tongues, in an unknown tongue, is the evidence that a person has received the baptism of the Holy Spirit and that the Spirit is living and dwelling inside the person.

The other teaching I want to clarify is this: some people put forth the doctrine that a person has to have been filled with the Spirit with the evidence of speaking in tongues in order to go to heaven. If that teaching were true, the man on the cross next to Jesus was not saved. This man, ...*said unto Jesus, Lord, remember me when thou comest into thy kingdom* (Luke 23:42). We know that he was saved because Jesus stated that he would be: *And Jesus said unto him, Verily I say unto thee, To day thou shalt be with me in paradise* (v. 43).

There is no evidence that the man, who Jesus said would be with Him in paradise, spoke in tongues. The day of Pentecost had not yet happened. That was the day, ...*they were all filled with the Holy Ghost, and began to speak with other tongues, as the Spirit gave them utterance* (Acts 2:4). Jesus would not send the Holy Ghost, the Comforter, until after He had gone away, until after He had departed through His death and resurrection. (See John 16:7; 7:39.) There have been many debates on the meaning of "paradise" and "heaven" and whether they are the same. I am not addressing that debate in this book because it is not relevant to my message on operating in the nine gifts of the Spirit. What is relevant is that if the doctrine is true that a person has to speak in tongues in order to go to heaven, probably no one before the day of Pentecost would have gone to heaven.

Believers who do speak in tongues need to be very careful about criticizing other believers in denominations which don't necessarily teach about the baptism of the Holy Spirit and speaking in tongues.

The Purpose of the Nine Gifts of the Spirit

Let's begin looking more specifically at the nine gifts of the Spirit and their operation. The purpose of the gifts is for us to use them in ministering to other people (and to ourselves as well, at times, which we will look at later). The gifts are given so that we have the *equipment* we need to minister.

Before Paul described the gifts in detail and defined their purpose, he began with the instruction not to be ignorant of them. If we don't realize that the gifts are available to us, we won't know how to draw on everything God has for us in order to walk in His fullness.

First Corinthians 12:1-4:

Now concerning spiritual gifts, brethren, I would not have you ignorant.

Ye know that ye were Gentiles, carried away unto these dumb idols, even as ye were led.

Wherefore I give you to understand, that no man speaking by the Spirit of God calleth Jesus accursed: and that no man can say that Jesus is the Lord, but by the Holy Ghost.

Now there are diversities of gifts, but the same Spirit.

This passage tells us there is diversity in the gifts. When we divide up the gifts and start looking at them, we find three categories. Three of them of them deal with revelation gifts, three with power gifts, and three with vocal gifts (or as some Bible teachers call them, "inspiration" gifts): three, three, and three.

When I am teaching, I use a candelabra to represent the golden lamp stand that was in the Tabernacle in the day of Moses (Exod. 26:35) as an image of our relationship with Jesus and our expression of the gifts and the fruit of the Holy Spirit in our lives.

Jesus said that He is the Vine and we are simply the branches. (John 15:5.) The piece in the center of the lamp stand, or candelabra in my demonstration, represents Jesus Christ who is our focus. The branches represent us, those who have received Jesus as Savior, coming out from Him. Any branch that could be broken off would break from the piece in the center. Jesus is also the Light. He is the Source of light in the candelabra. Because Jesus is the Light and He is in us and we are in Him, then we produce the light also. Isn't that good? The light we produce on the candelabra emanates from Him.

The golden lamp stand had six branches, three branches going out from each side of the center stem. (See Exod. 25:32.) At the top of each branch and the center stem was a candle. The lamp stand held seven candles, seven lights. The number seven in the Bible signifies the fullness of God.

Three little bud-like shapes—little cups like almond blossoms, each with a knob and a flower—were on each branch. (See Exod. 25:33 AMP.) The set of three branches going out from one side of the center stem presents an image of the diverse gifts emanating from the one Spirit. Each branch represents a category of the gifts of the Spirit with the three knobs on each branch representing the three gifts in each category—three, three, and three: the nine gifts. So now we have the seven branches representing the fullness of God and the three branches with nine knobs on one side of the center stem representing the nine gifts of the Spirit, which we need to operate in our lives in order to experience the fullness of God. However, so far the image is off balance. The set of three branches on the other side of the stem in the image we are looking at represents the qualities we need for balance in our lives: the nine fruit of the Spirit.

Balance

You have probably known people who were really on fire for God, really full of zeal, who operated in the gifts of the Spirit, turned the devil on his head, came through like a whirlwind for a few months or maybe even a few years, but then all of a sudden were gone. Do you know why? They didn't have any balance in their lives. The least little bit of wind that came along blew them over because their lives were off balance.

Jesus said that you are the salt of the earth and the light of the world. He said the light that you are should not be set under a bushel and hidden, but exposed. (Matt. 5:13-15.) The lamp stand in the holy place of the Tabernacle was to stay lit. (Lev. 24:4.) Many church folks don't understand that we are supposed to be shining our light twenty-four hours a day, seven days a week—not just on Sunday. And this takes balance in our lives, the balance of operating in the gifts of the Spirit while motivated by the fruit of the Spirit.

When people are out of balance from concentrating on operating in the nine gifts of the Spirit without giving any attention to growing up in the nine fruit of the Spirit, they topple over when the least little bit of wind comes along no matter how big a whirlwind they themselves seem to be. It hardly takes anything to blow them over and make them fall because they are off balance. Being off balance happens to many Christians. In this book I want to help people see how much of a need there is for bringing and maintaining balance in life. In order to remain steadfast, in order to consistently shine our lights, we need to give attention to balancing the gifts with the fruit. When the gifts become prevalent in our lives as balanced by the fruit, we will produce light.

The Fruit of the Spirit

Galatians 5:22-23 lists the nine fruit of the Spirit, the attributes God has put in His Spirit inside of us, for us to develop and draw on in order to keep our lives balanced: *But the fruit of the Spirit is love, joy, peace, longsuffering, gentleness, goodness, faith [faithfulness, NASB], meekness, temperance: against such there is no law.*

God gives us the gifts of the Spirit—we can't receive them by works. A gift isn't something we work for or buy. If we work for a gift, it isn't a gift. The Father gives us gifts because He loves us and because we're in the right place with Him. When we've received His Son Jesus and we open ourselves up to receiving God's gifts, we're in the right place with Him. The gifts of the Spirit come from the Father. Fruit, however, is something that grows from the seed residing in the Holy Spirit inside us.

We grow the fruit from the seed planted in us by guarding, developing, and nourishing that seed in order to display the mature fruit in our lives. We have to take care of that seed for it to grow properly. We have to dung it so it grows well. What does "dung it" mean? It means to fertilize or dress with dung; otherwise, the seed won't grow very well! We also plant seeds around us, by sowing them, to receive a harvest. We know from Galatians 6:7 that, ... *whatsoever a man soweth, that shall he also reap.* To produce the fruit of kindness in your life, for example, you will need to sow some in order to receive it. The gifts of the Spirit, God gives. The fruit of the Spirit, we grow.

God wants us to allow the gifts of the Spirit to flow through us to minister, but He also wants us to do it in a way that communicates His nature through displaying the fruit of His Spirit.

There are people who like to move in the gifts of the Spirit to look good or spiritual or to get attention. Because of pride or immaturity or a lack of knowledge, they seem to think the purpose for operating in the gifts is to be seen and heard! They are actually abusing the gifts, exploiting them in a measure, rather than ministering through them and are disregarding, or are ignorant of, the importance of displaying the fruit of the Spirit in their lives. They are motivated by pride, by the desire to feel important, rather than by the desire to move in the Spirit to minister to people. They are operating in the flesh.

God gives us a vivid example, through the Old Testament account of His direction for entering the Holy of Holies in the Tabernacle, of the important difference between operating under His anointing and operating in the flesh. The golden lamp stand, that we have been looking at as a representation of our relationship with Jesus and God's fullness available to us, was set up in the Holy Place outside the veil, the inner curtain that was hung as a separation from the Holy of Holies. (Lev. 24:3.) God's instructions were for the high priest to enter the Holy of Holies once a year to offer atonement for the people's sin. If any person tried to enter the Holy of Holies, including the high priest at any other time in any other way than the way God had designated for the Day of Atonement, that person would die. (See Lev. 16.)

The veil that kept everybody out of the Holy of Holies was made of *blue and purple and scarlet material and fine twisted linen...with cherubim, the work of a skillful workman* (Exod. 26:31 NASB). It didn't have a zipper in it; it didn't have a button in it, and the only way it could be passed through was by the supernatural anointing of God. We can imagine on that one day of the year, when the high priest was ready to enter the Holy of Holies, that God would just open up the curtain for the high priest to walk right into His glory. A candle did not need to be in the Holy of Holies because the glory of God lit the whole place. His presence was there. Everything He is was there. Divine healing was there. In His presence there would not be the need to pray for divine healing because He is divine health.

The only way a person could enter into God's presence was by the Spirit; any person who tried to enter the Holy of Holies in the flesh would die. In the same way, do you know what is keeping the church out of the glory of God today? It is called "flesh." The motivation to feel important rather than to move in the Spirit to minister to people is an example of walking according to the flesh.

The Lord wants us to operate in the gifts but out of the right motivation which comes from developing the fruit. First Corinthians 12:31 tells us, *But covet earnestly the best gifts: and yet shew I unto you a more excellent way.* Then Paul, in First Corinthians 13, described something more excellent than all nine of those gifts. He showed us the best gifts that we can earnestly covet and then said there is a more excellent way than those. Paul said that way is charity, love in action.

In First Corinthians 13:1-2, Paul described the importance of charity related to operating in the gifts of the Spirit.

Though I speak with the tongues of men and of angels, and have not charity, I am become as sounding brass, or a tinkling cymbal.

And though I have the gift of prophecy, and understand all mysteries, and all knowledge; and though I have all faith, so that I could remove mountains, and have not charity, I am nothing.

Paul said you can prophesy or speak in tongues, you can do all these things, but if you don't have charity, if you don't have love, you're as a sounding brass or a tinkling cymbal. In other words, anybody who doesn't have charity, or anybody moving in the gifts without charity, we could say is a ding-a-ling! Charity, or love, is the basis of the fruit of the Spirit. God is love, and all the other fruit come from love. Allowing God to develop His character and attributes in us through growing in His fruit, based in the fruit of love, gives us the right motivation to operate His gifts.

To walk in the fullness of God we need to focus on not just operating in the gifts of the Spirit but on growing and displaying the fruit of the Spirit.

2

Diversities of Gifts but the Same Spirit

We saw before in First Corinthians 12:4, *Now there are diversities of gifts, but the same Spirit.*

First Corinthians 12:5-7:

And there are differences of administrations, but the same Lord.

And there are diversities of operations, but it is the same God which worketh all in all.

But the manifestation of the Spirit is given to every man to profit withal.

These manifestations of the Spirit are given to every man to do what? To *profit withal* as translated in the *King James Version*.

A literal translation of verse 7 gives us additional insight into the meaning of *profit withal*. The manifestation of the Spirit is given in everything for us to be able to profit—in everything we do, we would be prospering. So in other words, *The Interlinear Bible* states: *But to each one is given the showing forth of the Spirit to our profit* (emphasis mine). Isn't that good? The manifestation of the Spirit is given for us to profit—to get ahead and to accomplish things in our lives, to succeed.

Galatians 5:16 gives us insight into how this works: *This I say then, Walk in the Spirit, and ye shall not fulfil the lust of the flesh.* The *New American Standard Bible* words the verse this way: *But I say, walk by the Spirit, and you will not carry out the desire of the flesh.* In other words, we are going to have desires and thoughts that are not always holy desires and thoughts, but if we will walk in the Spirit and allow the anointing of God to consume us, guess what? We won't carry out those desires. We won't carry out that lust of the flesh. We will prosper in all the things we do.

Something many people don't realize about living in the fullness of God through letting the gifts operate is this: we will not only have help in the present times of need and tough times, but the Spirit will show us things to come in our own lives. Many times people are trying to use the gifts to minister to everybody else but may not think about allowing the word of wisdom, for example, to reveal things to help them in their own future. Some people think the gift of discernment is given for them to see demons in other people. (With some folks, it doesn't take a supernatural gift of discernment to see they have a demon!) My point is that when we begin to be led by the Spirit in the gift of discernment, the Spirit will use that gift to reveal to us what is wrong with ourselves. He will show us things we are doing to cause ourselves trouble that keep us from receiving the Lord's help or healing, preventing us from walking in His fullness.

The Diverse Nine Gifts of the Spirit

First Corinthians 12:8-10:

For to one is given by the Spirit the word of wisdom; to another the word of knowledge by the same Spirit.

To another faith by the same Spirit; to another the gifts of healing by the same Spirit.

To another the working of miracles; to another prophecy; to another discerning of spirits; to another diverse kinds of tongues; to another the interpretation of tongues.

The gifts listed in the order of the Scripture passage are:

> the word of wisdom,
>
> the word of knowledge,
>
> faith by the same spirit,
>
> the gifts of healing,
>
> the working of miracles,
>
> prophecy,
>
> discerning of spirits,
>
> diverse kinds of tongues,
>
> the interpretation of tongues.

Some people may look at this list and not realize, for example, we are saved by faith, but there is also a gift of faith. Some people may say, "I'm saved, but I don't have faith." No, if you've been born again, you have faith. We are saved by faith. We have to have faith in order to be saved. But we need to understand that in addition to that kind of faith, there is a gift of faith.

Just as the faith to receive Jesus is different from the gift of faith, somebody speaking in tongues is functioning in a different way from someone giving a message in tongues as one of the gifts of the Spirit. Some people have not received very much teaching on this. I have heard some people make a comment about being in a service at a church and hearing someone speak in tongues but there wasn't any interpretation following. They were mistaking someone speaking in tongues for someone delivering a message through the gift of tongues. The only time there needs to be an interpretation is following a message of tongues delivered to a body of believers.

The Gifts Are Available to All

First Corinthians 12:11 and 12 shows us that God places these gifts in the body of Christ, and the Spirit divides them to every man as He wills. God has given each of us the ability to move in any of these gifts.

But all these worketh that one and the selfsame Spirit, dividing to every man severally as he will,

For as the body is one, and hath many members, and all the members of that one body, being many, are one body: so also is Christ.

We who are believers in Jesus are all temples of the Holy Ghost. First Corinthians 6:19: *What? know ye not that your body is the temple of the Holy Ghost which is in you, which ye have of God, and ye are not your own?* God has put the Holy Ghost and the availability of these gifts in each of us—in each temple, each tabernacle, each house. He has given each of us all these gifts.

Verse 11, *But all these worketh that one and the selfsame Spirit, dividing to every man severally as he will,* shows us that the gifts work in every person as the Spirit wills. There is another teaching that doesn't line up with the Bible which I want to put out here, one that is simply goofy. This teaching puts forth the idea that God drops certain gifts of the nine gifts into certain people in the church. One person is given one of the gifts, another person is given another of the gifts, and so on. If this teaching is true, what would happen if the person through whom the gifts of healing operates, for instance, couldn't be at a particular church service? Maybe the person was scheduled to work or is out deer hunting or something else. Those of us in church would be in a mess if we needed the gifts of healing to operate, wouldn't we? What if the person in the church with the gift of faith was gone and we needed the gift of faith operating in the service that night? That would be a difficult situation, and that is not the way the Spirit works. He manifests in any of us as He wills to meet different needs.

We are like the holy vessels described in the Tabernacle. In giving Moses the directions to build and establish the Tabernacle, the Lord told Moses to anoint the golden lamp stand and the other furnishings and vessels in the Tabernacle to make them holy. (Exod. 30:25-29.) *And thou shalt sanctify them, that they may be most holy: whatsoever toucheth them shall be holy* (Exod. 30:29). In one image, we were looking at Jesus as the Light of the lamp stand, or candelabra, and us as the light shining from Him. In a similar way, think of us as being like the anointed vessels in the Tabernacle that made holy anything (or anyone) touching them.

What this means is that we are the vessels of the Lord, and we are anointed for His use in the way He sees we need to be used in different instances. If you go to the hospital to pray for somebody who is sick, what does the sick person need? More than likely, the sick person needs the gifts of healing or the gift of miracles rather than the gift of tongues and interpretation to meet the need for healing! The sick person probably doesn't need the gift of discernment (that is, a misunderstanding of that gift with a comment such as, "I discern that if you hadn't eaten all that fried chicken, you wouldn't be in the hospital!") to meet the need. Those gifts are not needed at that time. But at other times the gift of discernment is needed to minister.

Because we are the vessels of the Lord, once we have been born again, we have the anointing of God. It is up to us to seek the gifts we desire to operate through us. There isn't just one gift that we operate in although one particular gift may frequently operate through us. In my church, my wife, Sharon, operates in the gifts of healing very beautifully. I like having her minister healing with me when I am praying for the sick because the gifts of healing flow so readily through her—I can feel the anointing. It's like at other times if you have to go fight out something with somebody, don't you like having somebody else with you as support? When I am ministering healing and fighting those sicknesses, I like to have her beside me.

Someone else, Matt, in my church—boy, does he know how to pray. He knows how to quote the Word of God. I like having him around me when I need the Word of God quoted.

What is important to understand is that we all have access to all nine of the gifts. The Holy Ghost doesn't work by giving one person the gift of faith and another person the gifts of healing and somebody else the gift of miracles then another person the gift of tongues to use. If we are going to walk in the fullness of God and be what He wants us to be, we need to know that we have access to any of the nine gifts we might need to minister in any situation.

It is true there may be some gifts that we favor or function in more frequently than others. In my church there are some people who flow really well in the gift of prophecy, others who flow really well in the gift of tongues, and others in other gifts. But again, we need all these gifts. We need to be available for the Holy Spirit to operate any one of them through us.

The gifts are weapons that we can use against the devil. The gifts are our security—our homeland security! We need these gifts of the Spirit.

God Places Ministry Gifts in the Church

God sets gifts in the body of believers in a church. God has all the gifts of the Spirit available to operate through all the people in the body, but He places the ministry gifts, the offices, the office of a senior pastor, for example, in a church because He doesn't need four senior pastors in one church.

First Corinthians 12:27-30 describes some of the ministry gifts in the body.

Now ye are the body of Christ and members in particular.

And God hath set some in the church, first apostles, secondarily prophets, thirdly teachers, after that miracles, then gifts of healings, helps, governments, diversities of tongues.

Are all apostles? are all prophets? are all teachers? are all workers of miracles?

Have all the gifts of healing? do all speak with tongues? do all interpret?

We can see the lengthy history of the ministry of helps that began back in the Tabernacle God instructed Moses to establish. The high priest Aaron was to tend the lamps on the golden lamp stand continually. (See Lev. 24:1-4.) Every day the lamp stand had to be cleaned. The oil and the light drew bugs to it. The lamp stand was not built for bugs and flies, and when they died, they fell in the oil. Every day the priest had to do two things to the lamp. He had to dip out the flies and the bugs and do away with them in order for the lamp not to smell and have a stink. Then he needed to make the light as bright as possible by trimming the wick. In other words, he saw to it that light burned bright.

God wanted the light to burn bright, and do you know what He wants out of you? He wants you to burn bright. He wants us to burn bright like the lamp stand, and He also wants us to take care of the lamp stand to help others burn bright. This is the place where the ministry of helps comes in. The ministry of helps is you and me. It is all of us.

People who I never dreamed would hear about the church I pastor have been hearing about it because the church burns bright. New Beginnings Church burns as bright as it does because so many of the people in it are burning bright. We've done away with a lot of smelly, stinking things. We've dealt with the flesh and we keep dealing with it. We get rid of those things that are dead in our lives, and we keep trimming the wick, causing the light to shine bright. Recently we took a truckload of boxes to meet a need in Oklahoma City because the people in my church serve in the ministry of helps as needed and they are burning bright.

Not everyone will go up to the front of the church and prophesy; not everyone will go up to the front of the church and pray for the sick; not everyone will help raise the dead. Not everyone will do these things. But all the people play their part. All do what they can. God places the gifts to meet the needs as the Spirit wills. He will set one senior pastor in a church, but the ministry of helps is for all the people in the church.

Let's look again at First Corinthians 12:31: *But covet earnestly the best gifts: and yet shew I unto you a more excellent way.*

Notice that "gifts" is plural, not "gift," singular. After Paul talks about the importance of having charity to operate in the gifts of the Spirit, what charity is and how it behaves itself, he says to desire spiritual "gifts," plural: *Follow after charity, and desire spiritual gifts…*(1 Cor. 14:1).

People who don't desire the gifts won't have to worry about the gifts operating in their lives. If they don't desire the gifts to operate, God is not going to say something like, "Hey, I'm going to make you operate in the gifts of healing." No. He won't make you operate in that gift or in any of the other gifts. If you don't want to operate in the working of miracles, for example, there won't be any miracles happening.

Soon I will have been in thirty-something foreign countries, and every time I go into a foreign country and start praying for people, do you know what happens? Miracles, miracles, miracles. Why? Because the people in those countries believe that miracles are going to happen. I love seeing those miracles—it is exciting to me. But I have to want those miracles to happen or else they won't happen. And I have to be open to any of the diverse nine gifts of the Spirit operating through me. One way we walk in God's fullness is by allowing the Holy Spirit to express His diversity in the ways He wills to flow through us.

3

Operating in the Strength of the Spirit

It is God's desire that we be filled with the Spirit and that we begin to operate on the strength of His Spirit. Being filled with the Spirit is more than just a suggestion. It is actually a commandment. Ephesians 5:18 says *And be not drunk with wine, wherein is excess; but be filled with the Spirit.*

We are living in a society that wants to just barely get by. We are living in the days that fit the Bible description of the last days, and as I mentioned earlier, there have been tough times and there will be more tough times. The types of things that are coming in the last days are bringing times when we need to be fearless.

I want you to understand that being filled with the Spirit is what will help carry us through victoriously. If I had a glass full of water, there would not be room for anything else. We can begin to realize that we can be full of the Spirit of God, and there won't be room for anything else.

Operating in the Strength of the Spirit Brings Success

As we looked at before in First Corinthians 12:4-6, it is the same God who works all in all in the diversities of gifts, the differences of administrations, and the diversities of operations, and in verse 7, *But the manifestation of the Spirit is given to every man to profit withal.* In everything you do these gifts are to help you to profit—as we saw, to get ahead, to accomplish, to succeed.

When we hear teaching about this passage, we hear that God gives the gifts to us to minister to other people. Of course, this is very true. But I am going to make a statement here that needs to be read carefully and not taken out of context: we need to be able to use the gifts in our own lives first before we go out there and use them on other people. We need to operate the gifts for ourselves in our own lives because we must understand that if something isn't good enough for ourselves, we don't need to be preaching it to somebody else. If we can't live by something, we need to stop trying to get everybody else to live by it.

The Spirit Brings Life

I was raised up in a godly home with godly principles, and I appreciate that I was. But for years as I was growing up, we lived by a set of laws and principles that were laid out. These laws were so stringent that even the pastors couldn't live by them. Then what would happen is that after a while, the pastors would throw in the towel. Why? The Apostle Paul tells us. He said the law, the letter of the law, kills: *...for the letter killeth, but the spirit giveth life*

(2 Cor. 3:6). If the pastors couldn't live by these laws and rules themselves, how could they expect the people in the congregation to live by them? This is an example of why I am saying that we need to be able to use the gifts of the Spirit for ourselves, applying them to ourselves, before we go out and try to minister to others with them.

In the church I grew up in, we had so many rules, we backslid a lot. Some folks may say that they don't believe in backsliding. Around my church, we did! Sometimes we backslid three times a week. Usually, I backslid more. Until I was fifteen years old, I backslid. I started off by backsliding after Sunday morning service. One of my friends usually came home with me after Sunday morning church, and he and I would get into a disagreement over something then I would start calling him names. After that I prayed through to repent and get right with God again. Then Sunday and Wednesday nights I backslid again. Each time after I backslid, I prayed through. I prayed through after services Sunday morning, Sunday night, and Wednesday night. Then I would backslide again between Wednesday night and Sunday night.

When I was in college, I wasn't perfect either. I went to college for two and a half years, but my major is no longer good in my life because I majored in hall: study hall, pool hall, and alcohol! But I've been born again, hallelujah, and I don't live like I did live. All that is under the blood of Jesus.

When I was growing up in church, those services used to last and last and last. They went on and on and on because the way we did things in my church, people didn't get filled with the Holy

Ghost until past midnight. Forget about this eight o'clock stuff! It was like those people were operating on that Energizer battery!

Our church had wood floors built up off the ground. In those days, the ladies wore those really high heels, those 6-inch spiked shoes. One of my grandmothers weighed about 350 pounds. My great grandmother weighed only about 300 pounds. She was a lightweight. My grandmothers and my mother were the shouters and the dancers in the church. One of my grandmothers used to sit way up there on the front row, and we knew she was starting to get with praising and worshipping the Lord when we began to hear the click of those high heels on that wood floor.

In those days, we didn't have a nursery for the kids. We didn't even know that some churches had nurseries! The kids who went outside did so for one of two reasons: to either get dinner or a whopping. So I slept under the pew. That may sound hard to do, but we were used to extreme conditions. My family lived out in western Oklahoma, and when I went to school, I walked a half mile uphill to the bus stop. It was cold out in western Oklahoma because there was nothing to block the wind. The snow was deep, and in hot weather, the days and nights were really hot.

My biggest fear growing up as a child in the church sleeping under the pew in those late night services was when the high heels of the shouters and the dancers started going on that wooden floor. My Grandma McGregor was in front of me and my momma was right there on the same pew with me, and I was lying on the hard wood floor asleep. I always slept in a way to fit under the pew. I might turn over and on my stomach and tuck my hands under me. My greatest fear was that after I fell asleep, one of my hands would fall out from under the pew onto the floor right under one of those high heels in action. During those three-week revivals, I actually had nightmares. I would go home every night and dream, "What if my hand gets nailed?"

The set of laws and principles we lived by carried into every part of our lives. Even the way the ladies wore their hair reflected the strict rules. The way we looked at it in those days, God didn't let the women cut their hair. Because we thought it was a sin for women to cut their hair, what the women did to shorten their hair was burn it off! They grabbed their hair and held it over a flame on the stove. One of my relatives wanted her hair a little shorter and decided a good way to do that would be to wad it up in a knot and use a fan to whack it off! Needless to say, after she finished using the fan to create her new hairdo, the lesson to everyone else was, "Don't do that!"

Nobody could live by the set of stringent rules the church had made that the pastor expected everybody else to live by but he couldn't even live by himself. In the same way, if we expect to be able to minister in the gifts of the Spirit to other people, we need to make sure we are walking in the Spirit to the point that He is able to minister the gifts to us in our own lives first.

Another thing that I want to point out is this: I run into many people who say something like this, "I don't want to go to church because my mom and dad made me go to church all the time. I was raised having to go to church, and I'm not going to put myself or my family through that." What the people who are making these types of comments are missing is the importance of raising a family in a way that shows and teaches commitment to God.

As I said, the church I grew up in had so many laws and principles that nobody could follow them. The church wasn't perfect, but as I also said, I am glad my family made sure I was raised in church. The whole time I was growing up, if the doors to the church were open, if there was nothing more than a prayer meeting going on, we were there. I never ever heard my mom or dad say, "Do you think we ought to go to church today?" Whether we would go to church or not was never a question. We never took a vacation.

I am not saying that you should never take a vacation and miss church—not at all. I believe in taking vacations. When I take a vacation, I don't necessarily go to church. But what I'm saying is this: a parent who raises a family without a commitment to attend church is just making an excuse of some kind. For one thing, there are many good churches, churches full of the life of God, out there to raise a family in that are very different from the type of church a parent may have attended growing up. Even though, growing up, I wasn't perfect and we in the church weren't perfect and the set of rules my church followed wasn't perfect, I grew up in a home committed to serving God. My parents instilled that value in me by making sure I was raised in church.

Living a Victorious Life through the Strength of the Spirit

In my example of a church that tries to live by such letter-of-the-law rules that the pastor can't even follow them and leaves the ministry, the letter of the law killed. Trying to follow a set of rules for their own sake, or for tradition's sake, has nothing to do with following the Spirit and doesn't bring life. What we need to understand is the Spirit of God comes to give us life and make us able to live a victorious life through His strength no matter what is going on around us. We need to be filled with His Spirit, follow Him, and follow the teaching in the Bible, not a set of made-up rules.

The Nine Gifts Are for Everyday Living

The nine gifts of the Spirit are for everyday living. If you are operating in the nine gifts at home and you come to church, guess what? You will operate in the nine gifts at church. If the gift of faith is operating in me at home, then when I come to church, the gift of faith will operate through me at church. When I gather together with the body of believers in Christ and I already have been operating in the gift of faith, or the working of miracles, at home, when I go to church and we pray for one another, guess what? The gift of faith operates through me and miracles can happen.

Because we're living in a microwave age, people tend to think they can make demands on God as if we're dialing one of these free 800 numbers. In some ways being able to dial an 800 number for someone to pray for us has been a real detriment to the church. It has been easy for us to dial a number for prayer rather than getting on our knees and praying and interceding for ourselves.

I've been around television ministries for many years and some—I don't mean this to be a blanket statement, that's why I say *some*, not *all*—of those 800 numbers you call for prayer gather the names and mailing addresses into a computer database and sell them as mailing lists. Where do you think some of those magazine companies that you receive mail from get your name?

Let me emphasize that I am not saying to never call 800 numbers for prayer. Not every ministry sells names and addresses as mailing lists. Some ministries have 800 numbers available to call for prayer for just that: prayer. But quite a few do sell information as mailing lists. I have done telethons for some of the biggest ministry organizations, and I have seen this happen. Again some, not all, do this. But my point is that we in the body of Christ need to quit being so gullible and ignorant, and instead, understand that what God is trying to do is be who He wants to be in our lives. What He wants to do is fill us up with His Spirit and His anointing so that when we have the gifts of healing or the working of miracles or faith, or any other of the nine gifts of the Spirit operating in our lives, and we walk in them, we don't have to rely on anyone else for God to move in our lives. The church needs to understand that we are complete in Him. We are not complete in anything else. We are not complete in a mate, in a church facility we finished building, in a job, or in an automobile. Those things don't make us complete. You and I are complete only when we are complete in Him.

God wants His Spirit to start working in a mighty way in our local churches. When we become born again, we become vessels that become the work of the Lord. When we become born again, God wants to fill us with His Spirit because He wants to fill us up with all that He is.

In Matthew 16:19, Jesus talks about the keys to the kingdom: *And I will give unto thee the keys of the kingdom of heaven: and whatsoever thou shalt bind on earth shall be bound in heaven: and whatsoever thou shalt loose on earth shall be loosed in heaven.*

Jesus has given us the keys to the kingdom. What is a key? A device to enable us to have access to a locked position. I believe those keys to the kingdom are the nine gifts of the Spirit—any one of the nine gifts is a key. It goes back to grace—God gives us these gifts freely. What God is trying to do through giving us the gifts is give us the keys to the kingdom. He wants us to take the gifts and use them as keys. When we receive these gifts, then we have access to the things that the enemy, Satan, has tried to keep locked up to prevent us from experiencing the fullness of God's kingdom.

When we have the key of faith or the key of healing or the key of miracles, we can gain access to the things the enemy is trying to keep locked away from us. When this became a revelation to me, I became excited because I understood that I have access to everything God has and everything He is. I understood the verse that says, *No weapon that is formed against thee shall prosper...*(Isa. 54:17) to mean much, much more than I ever had because it means I have faith, I have healing, I have miracles, and all the other gifts operating as a part of my life because God freely gave them to me.

Jesus said He will give us "the keys," plural, "of the kingdom of heaven." He didn't say He would give us one key of the kingdom; He said "keys." All the gifts of the Spirit are accessible to us—all of them.

God has freely given these gifts to us to use as keys to access the things He has for us. He wants us to receive them and use them in our everyday living so that we can walk in His fullness in our lives and minister that fullness to others. We need to use the keys to keep the devil under our feet and locked out of things God has for us. I want to keep the devil in a place that the only thing he can get out of me is to read the bottom of my boot! God wants us to unlock and access all He has for us and others through us for us all to enjoy the benefits of His kingdom.

4

The Revelation Gifts, the Power Gifts, and the Vocal Gifts

To walk in the fullness of God and live from the strength of His Spirit, God has given us of the nine gifts of the Spirit in the three categories: the revelation gifts, the power gifts, and the vocal (or "inspiration") gifts.

The Revelation Gifts

The revelation gifts contain the word of wisdom, the word of knowledge, and the discerning of spirits. The word of wisdom is for our future. It is to help us in our future so that we can prosper, profit. It is to help us with our lives. The word of knowledge is for the present time: for now. God gives us a gift of knowledge for now. Remember, *all* the gifts are given for us to *profit withal*: to succeed. The discerning of spirits lets us know, or shows us, the difference between truth and error. One way this gift helps us is to know how to make the right decisions to lead us in a way that results in us prospering and being blessed. These gifts reveal something.

The Power Gifts

The power gifts contain (the gift of) faith, the gifts of healing, and the working of miracles. The gift of faith is faith to do the extraordinary, a faith to go beyond what the natural man is able to do. Notice that the "gifts" of healing is plural. There is more than one kind of healing, and this gift releases the energy to bring healing for all the types needed. It is God's power flowing through someone's body to drive out afflictions—*all* our diseases, *all* our sicknesses. The working of miracles is a supernatural manifestation of God's ability, the ability of God exhibited above the natural, an act of God. Miracles are not limited to healing; they have to do with anything that pertains to life and godliness. As with all the other gifts, this gift is supernatural. If we can accomplish something or do it, then it is not a miracle. We will never be able to figure out a miracle; we will never be able to figure out how it happened.

These three gifts hold power and produce power (or energy). They hold power, energy, that when released, do something. They are in us to use to accomplish things. I love the story about the balloon salesman that expresses an important point about the power available to us from the Spirit inside of us. You've probably seen balloon salesmen at a carnival. They have a hand full of helium-filled balloons on strings.

One day, when business was slow for a balloon salesman at a carnival, he let off into the air a blue balloon to attract everybody's attention for them to start thinking about buying balloons again. Then after a little while He let off a white balloon, then a yellow one, then a red one. A little boy watching him noticed that he had never let off a black balloon.

The little boy went over to the salesman and said, "Sir, I watched you today. You let off a blue balloon, a white one, a yellow one, a red one—all the colors—except for a black balloon. Do the black balloons rise up and fly away, too?"

The balloon salesman said, "Son, remember this: it isn't the color of the balloon that causes it to rise; it's what's on the inside of that balloon that causes it to rise." I submit to you that it isn't the color of your skin or the denomination you came out of or are in; it isn't your ancestors and it isn't who you used to be—it's what is on the inside of you right now that will cause you to rise or fall. Something that God is going to do in the body of Christ is to get His church full of the Spirit so that we in the church can rise up. It doesn't matter what other religions—the Muslims, any other "Isms"—or what the antichrist is doing or will do. Know this: God wants us to be filled with His Spirit so that we can rise up and be seen by the world so that the world can know that Jesus Christ lives on the inside of us.

We know from Malachi 3: *And all the nations shall call you blessed: for ye shall be a delightsome land.* In these last days, God is wanting us to let His Spirit dwelling on the inside of us to rise up. He wants us walking in His fullness so that people can look at us and call us blessed. Isn't that good to know? Don't we all want that?

This is so important for us, the church: we need something on the inside of us that causes the world to want what we have. For people who want just to warm the pew once a week and live the way they want to live the rest of the time, church-going is boring. They don't know what it's like to experience the power of God, and they are missing out on living in the fullness of God. I started New Beginnings almost nine years ago because the churches I had found were filled with a lot of rules, a bunch of do's and don'ts. There was no power in any of them, and I was tired of going to churches that didn't have the life or power of God in them.

Nobody was getting healed or saved or filled with the Holy Ghost. Nothing was happening except for people to come just to pay fire insurance—to make sure they stayed out of hell. I was sick of it. I could hardly sit in the church pew for the entire length of the message because there wasn't anything there but a drama. After my wife and I left one church we attended, my wife said, "Boy, that preacher should be in Hollywood because he sure wasn't a preacher." He was empty. I believe that God has more for us and wants more out of us than we have ever tapped into.

He wants us to begin to understand that He wants us full of faith; He wants us full of healing power; He wants us full of miracle power. Matt, I mentioned before who really knows how to pray, borrowed one of my books—*Miracle Workers, Reformers, and the New Mystics* by John Crowder (Shippensburg: Destiny Image® Publishers, Inc., 2006, pp. 52-55)—about the supernatural, about miraculous things. He was all excited reading about the men in the account who said they would not raise a hand against a brother in Christ.

The book tells of the Roman emperor Maximian Caesar who, in the third century A.D., told men of God serving under him to put down a rebellion among the Gauls, north of the Alps in Switzerland near the city of Thebes, by slaying some of the people who were not reverencing him in the way he wanted to be reverenced. The men of God came back and said the people who refused to reverence the emperor were brothers in Christ and they would not lay hands on them and kill them. Every one of the 6,600 men sent to destroy the Christian brothers refused to harm them. As a result, those warriors gave their own lives.

This account, including and especially the following part, is not exclusively in a book about historical events related to Christianity written by a Christian; it appears in history books about Zurich.

There is a coat of arms and seal of Zurich today showing three of the martyred saints holding their own heads. It illustrates a historical event. The three saints depicted had been beheaded. The reason the coat of arms shows the three holding their own heads is that each body, after falling to the ground, got up, reached down and picked up its own head, walked away, and prayed! This is a recorded historical fact—it actually happened. I told Matt, "Wouldn't it be wonderful if all of us in the body of Christ had hold of that principle: no matter what it looks like may happen, we are not about to put a hand against a brother." Those men weren't the type of empty Christians who warm pews once a week. They were completely in tune with the Holy Ghost.

I believe we will really have to be full of the Holy Ghost in order to make a decision like those men made. The way I understand the Bible is to anticipate there is coming a day that the men and women on this planet earth will have to make a choice of equal weight: either they will chose to receive the mark of the beast or they will not receive it no matter what someone plans to do to them. Unless we have the Spirit of God living in us and rising up, we will never have the boldness to say, "I am going to die for Christ." In some churches today, it is hard to find anybody who will live for Him, let alone anybody who will die for Him.

The kind of display of power the Holy Spirit is capable of we are looking at in the above account, or any way the Holy Spirit rises up in us and manifests through His nine gifts, makes the world want what we have.

To summarize how the power gifts operate, they exert power or energy to do something. They get something done.

The Vocal Gifts

The vocal ("inspiration") gifts contain prophecy, diverse kinds of tongues, and the interpretation of tongues. Prophecy is an utterance that comes out of our spirit, not our intellect or head knowledge, for edification, exhortation, and comfort—to build up and lift up—spoken to the church. It is birthed out of our spirit man and then uttered. We need to be careful not to "prophesy" in the flesh because this moves from prophecy to fortune-telling. There is also an office of a prophet, whose prophecy is most generally directed to a specific person, problem, or situation and toward the future. The office of the prophet is different from flowing as the Spirit wills in the gift of prophecy to the church.

Diverse kinds of tongues and the interpretation of tongues refer to a message in an unknown tongue by one person that is interpreted usually by another person. The message is speaking the mysteries of God, the secret things of God, an utterance of the Holy Ghost, that comes out of a person's spirit, not from the intellect, as the Spirit wills also for the benefit of the body of believers. The person's spirit is praying, but the person's understanding is unfruitful. The interpretation comes out of a person's spirit being, as well, and makes the message fruitful. Sometimes people give a message in tongues then give their own interpretation. Sometimes two or three people can have the same interpretation.

God gives us these nine gifts, these keys of the kingdom, so that we can do the *supernatural*, not something we could do naturally in our own abilities, through them. This is the reason every man, woman, boy, and girl need to be filled with the Holy Ghost and operate in the gifts of the Spirit: for Him to put us over so that we can be victorious in this world.

5

The Word of Wisdom

The book of Proverbs teaches that wisdom is very, very important. Proverbs 9:10 states: *The fear of the Lord is the beginning of wisdom....* Proverbs tells us to seek after and incline our ears to wisdom. Many times we gain wisdom about how to handle something coming up in the future in the natural way, by experiences. Understand, however, the word of wisdom is information gained from the Spirit *supernaturally* about our future. A word of wisdom is a small fragment of the mind of God. So what God does in giving a supernatural word of wisdom is speak something to help us in our future.

This supernatural gift of a word of wisdom comes in two different ways. The first way is directly from the Holy Ghost. In other words the Holy Ghost will speak a word of wisdom to us, to our spirit. The second way is through a human being. Often I hear people make the statement, "Well, I'm not going to receive this word unless God tells me. Bless God, I'm waiting on God to speak."

The problem with this is many times God gives us a word of wisdom through another person without directly telling us the same thing at the same time. If we don't have enough wisdom to be open to receiving a word of wisdom from somebody else, we will be in trouble. The reason we make dumb mistakes sometimes is that we won't receive a word of wisdom from somebody else.

God gives the pastor of a church a word of wisdom that will help the church touch people's lives and accomplish His purposes. For my church, as I pray and seek God's supernatural wisdom, He reveals and speaks direction to me in this way. This isn't just the wisdom of man I am receiving; I am receiving the wisdom of Almighty God, God's wisdom. With that wisdom God has given me, I make decisions that will cause my church to prosper.

Sometimes people in a church who hear the pastor reveal the wisdom God has given him think he didn't really hear from God because God didn't tell them the same thing. They should learn from Moses' example. Moses led around two million people out of bondage without God telling any one of those people how He was going to do it. He simply told Moses. He gave Moses a word of wisdom. Some people become rebellious and say, "Bless God, if God doesn't speak to me the same thing the pastor said He spoke to him, I'm not going to do it—I don't care what Pastor says." God's power isn't anything to brag about. God's power is to live and demonstrate. We need to realize when we are being rebellious and stop.

Psalm 50:23 says, *Whoso offereth praise glorifieth me: and to him that ordereth his conversation aright will I shew the salvation of God.* How are we going to order our conversation right if we don't have wisdom? Knowledge teaches us to talk and to walk, but wisdom teaches us how. It is very important to remember above everything else that we are here as the body of Christ to help people.

We are here to help God win the world. We are not here to help the devil! It is possible to really goof people up—confuse them and get them going in the wrong direction—when we don't use wisdom. How many people have come and gone through the doors of many churches and never come back because those churches were operating without drawing on God's wisdom? Parents understand the importance of wisdom. If they are raising children, they had better have some wisdom about them.

Godly Wisdom in Planning

Sometimes in the church world, people mistakenly think they shouldn't plan. They say, "Well, we want to be led by the Spirit, bless God." They think they should just go by what the Spirit does. They think the Spirit of God in all of His majesty and His ability can't plan! In a similar way of thinking, many preachers have scolded me because I use notes to preach. They tell me, "I tell you what, you just need to preach by the Holy Ghost. You don't need any notes." With this type of thinking, many times people are just reacting out of impulse, reacting out of their emotions, and guess what? Our emotions will goof us up. We need a word of wisdom.

Many churches don't function properly because the pastors never seek God for a word of wisdom. They say, "We just let the Spirit of God do what He wants to around here." This type of thinking is way off base. God wants to direct our lives and direct the church. He has a plan for the church. If a church doesn't look for a word of wisdom from Him, more than likely, that church will not have what He wants for it in the future.

Decisions Based on God's Wisdom

If Jesus needed wisdom, if it was important to His life, we can certainly see that we also need God's wisdom. Describing Jesus, Isaiah 11:1-2 says: *And there shall come forth a rod out of the stem of Jesse, and a Branch shall grow out of his roots: And the spirit of the LORD shall rest upon him, the spirit of wisdom and understanding, the spirit of counsel and might, the spirit of knowledge and of the fear of the LORD.* The Spirit of wisdom shall rest upon Him.

Acts 2:17 tells us, *And it shall come to pass in the last days, saith God, I will pour out of my Spirit upon all flesh....* This is a quotation of Joel 2:28. Part of God pouring out His Spirit upon us in these last days will be through the church doing signs and wonders and miracles. But I believe a major part will be that God will pour out of His Spirit, the manifestation of the Spirit of wisdom because, in the conditions surrounding us in the last days, we will need to have special wisdom in order to function victoriously in our daily living. We will need the Spirit of wisdom to know how to handle certain situations.

I have observed that the church world is nothing like it used to be even two, five, or ten years ago. The way to grow a church is not the same. In the eighties, I could grow a church of a hundred or more people in a year. But things are different now. We can't go to a conference and learn how to grow a church anymore. We can't put a sign up on the highway saying we're having revival and draw people anymore. People are not attracted to churches in the same way and by the same means they once were.

If we are going to grow a church today that will touch people's lives and be effective in our community, we need to be led by God's wisdom and have a church that is filled with the Spirit of wisdom.

Moved by Wisdom

I don't know how many times I have read through the first few verses of Isaiah 11, but about three o'clock one morning I saw something in verse 3 about living by the wisdom of God I became so excited over, I had a little Holy Ghost celebration right on the spot. I wanted to wake up my wife to tell her and celebrate again.

As we read in verses 1 and 2, resting on Jesus will be:

the spirit of the LORD

and *the spirit of wisdom and understanding*

and *the spirit of counsel and might*

and *the spirit of knowledge and of the fear of the LORD.*

Isaiah 11:3 goes on to tell us that these characteristics of the Spirit resting on Jesus, *...shall make him of quick understanding in the fear of the LORD: and he shall not judge after the sight of his eyes, neither reprove after the hearing of his ears.*

He is filled with the Spirit, and the Spirit of wisdom is upon Him so that He shall not judge after the sight of his eyes. He will judge by the Spirit of wisdom—not by the things He sees with His eyes! In other words, He will not be moved by what He sees.

He will be moved only by the instruction the wisdom of God gives Him! I had never seen this or heard anybody teach on this before.

Obviously, today we rely on the wisdom in the Word, especially Jesus' teaching later recorded in the New Testament after His death and resurrection, as well as the Spirit of wisdom. Some people can go off in a goofy direction if they don't base their decisions and actions on the Word as well the Spirit. But can you imagine where the church of Spirit-filled believers would go in the Spirit realm by focusing our attention on seeking after wisdom instead of judging and making decisions only by what we see and hear and by what other people are telling us? Can you imagine where we Spirit-filled believers would go in the Spirit realm if we were moved by the Spirit of wisdom instructing us instead of by our own judgment of what we should do?

Jesus' Wisdom

Here is an illustration of Jesus in action when He was moved by wisdom rather than by the things He saw with His eyes. John 8 gives us the account of the woman caught in adultery who was brought to Jesus. The circumstance that Jesus knew and saw was that according to the law, when a woman was caught in adultery, she was to be stoned to death. The scribes and the Pharisees said to Jesus, ...*this woman was taken in adultery, in the very act. Now Moses in the law commanded us, that such should be stoned: but what sayest thou?* (John 8:4-5). They were doing this to tempt Jesus that they might be able to accuse Him. (v. 6.)

But Jesus, having the Spirit of wisdom upon Him, was moved by wisdom rather than by the circumstance He saw. He was full of compassion, and the compassion that He had was moved by wisdom, His wisdom from God. Instead of judging her, instead of destroying and killing her, Jesus out of wisdom responded with this: let's not stone her. He said, ...*He that is without sin among you, let him first cast a stone at her* (v. 7).

I am not aware of another time in the Bible that an incident like this happened. Jesus was not copying what someone else had done; He was not following a precedent. He received revelation of what God would like to do in this particular woman's case and was moved by that wisdom.

For churches that operate by a set of rules of empty do's and don'ts, I wonder how many people have been destroyed? How many people have been killed? How many people have been cast out of the churches simply because the letter of the law of the particular church or denomination dictated dealing with something a certain way?

If we would quit judging by our eyesight, if we would quit judging by what we think, but instead be moved by the wisdom of God, we would bring restoration to many men and women who are coming through our church doors. We need to be working side by side with other brothers and sisters in Christ in this. In the example in John 8, here is a woman who, if the natural course of events had been followed, should have already been half dead. She should have been knocked in the head several times by huge rocks. But the Spirit of wisdom moved upon Jesus, and the Spirit of wisdom instructed Him to stoop down and write with his finger on the ground as though He didn't hear the question the scribes and the Pharisees were asking Him to try to accuse and entrap Him. The Spirit of wisdom moved upon Him to say to them that whichever of them was without sin, let him cast the first stone. (See vv. 6-7.)

From this account, we see what the Spirit of wisdom will do. That woman remained alive and was forgiven of her sins simply because the Spirit of wisdom moved upon Jesus. Are there people around us whom we have allowed to be destroyed? How many children, grandchildren, loved ones, or work friends have been destroyed because people have said such things as, "They ought to have enough sense to leave that dope alone." Obviously, they don't have enough sense to leave the dope alone. That is the reason they need somebody with wisdom to counsel and love them through the problem to find deliverance on the other side. Evidently the woman caught in adultery did not have enough sense to not commit adultery. We need to understand that not everybody knows how to make right decisions, or has enough sense to make the decisions that will affect their future for the positive.

Solomon's God-Given Wisdom

First Kings 3 tells of the wisdom of King Solomon. When Solomon became king, he asked the Lord, *Give therefore thy servant an understanding heart to judge thy people, that I may discern between good and bad...*(v. 9). In response to Solomon's request, God gave him *a wise and an understanding heart* (v. 12) so that there was not another man on earth with such great wisdom before or has been after. The wisdom of Solomon was legendary to the degree that ...*when the queen of Sheba heard of the fame of Solomon concerning the name of the LORD...*(1 Kings 10:1), she came to meet Solomon just to see him exhibit his wisdom for herself. She responded by saying the report of his acts and wisdom was true, and the half had not been told her; his wisdom and prosperity exceeded the fame she had heard. (1 Kings 10:6-7.)

We see another example of God's wisdom in action through the decision Solomon made to settle a dispute between two women living together in the same house, each claiming the same baby as hers. (1 Kings 3.) Both women had babies, but one woman lay on her baby in the night and it died. The woman who lost her baby exchanged it for the woman's live baby. Solomon, using God's wisdom, asked for a sword and said, ...*divide the living child in two, and give half to the one, and half to the other* (v. 25). He caused the real mother to want to save her baby. She said, *O my lord, give her the living child, and in no wise slay it...*(v. 26). Out of his wisdom he then knew which woman was the baby's mother. Wisdom saved that baby; wisdom saved the woman in adultery.

When the world looks upon us as Christians in the last days and calls us blessed, as I referred to in the Malachi 3:12 verse, many people think this means people in the world will look at our diamond rings, our new cars, our new houses, and other material possessions and call us blessed because we have many riches and other evidences of wealth. It could be that what people in the world are really going to look at is our wisdom, because driving a brand new car these days isn't evidence of wealth or that the owner is blessed. A person driving a new car may not even have good credit. It's very possible that the nations will rise up and call us blessed because of the godly wisdom they see us using to make decisions that cause us to *profit withal*, to be blessed with success and prosperity.

The Prophet Elisha's Wisdom from God

Second Kings 6 gives us another instance of action taken based upon God's wisdom. God used the prophet Elisha to warn the king of Israel not to send the Israelite army to a particular place where the Syrians, led by their king who was warring against Israel, would be. (vv. 8-10.) The king of Israel avoided an ambush by this same army more than once after God sent warnings through Elisha. God warned the Israelites by giving the prophet Elisha a word of wisdom for their future not to go to that place. The Israelites would have been in terrible trouble if their king had listened to anything but God's wisdom.

The next part of the account illustrates the word of knowledge in operation (the gift that we will look at in detail in the next chapter). The king of the enemy became enraged because he thought there was a spy in his camp telling the Israelites what they were doing. (v. 11.) This was the answer he received: *One of his servants said, "No, my lord, O king; but Elisha, the prophet who is in Israel, tells the king of Israel the words that you speak in your bedroom"* (v. 12 NASB).

One of the king of Syria's lowly servants was the one to inform him that the problem wasn't in their camp because the Israelites had a prophet in their land who, by the wisdom of God, told them when the king of Syria was going in and out, even knowing and telling them what was going on in his bed chamber! Elisha was operating in the word of knowledge by telling the king of Israel what was happening right then.

The next part of the account in 2 Kings 6 gives us a vivid example of being moved by God's wisdom—by His wisdom and knowledge, being moved by the spiritual reality—rather than being moved by what we judge initially with our eyes. The king of Syria gave the command to go to Dothan and take Elisha, and sent a great army by night that surrounded the city (vv. 13-14.)

Elisha's servant, after arising the next morning, was probably on his way to get his Old Testament equivalent of his Starbucks cup of coffee when he looked out and saw all the Syrians. After reacting with something like, "Wow! Where did all those Syrians come from?" he went right away to tell the prophet they were in deep trouble.

Verses 15-16 (NASB):

...And his servant said to him, "Alas, my master! What shall we do?"

So he answered, "Do not fear, for those who are with us are more than those who are with them."

The prophet began to pray for God to open his servant's eyes so that he could see how it really was.

Verse 17:

Then Elisha prayed and said, "O LORD, I pray, open his eyes that he may see." And the LORD opened the servant's eyes and he saw; and behold, the mountain was full of horses and chari-ots of fire all around Elisha.

It is amazing how we tend to think when times are going right that God knows what He is doing, but when we are in trouble and things are not going right, we think, *Where's God?* Elisha's servant told Elisha, "We're surrounded by the enemy; we're in big trouble; we've had it. I saw the army with my own eyes." But Elisha answers, "No, you just can't see well. There are more of us than there are of them."

We saw that Jesus followed the Spirit of wisdom instead of judging with His eyes and acting on that basis. Jesus judged by the wisdom of God. And if we haven't already learned to be like Him and judge on that basis, we need to do that. We need to learn to judge by what God says: ...*If God be for us, who can be against us?* (Rom. 8:31) and, ...*greater is he that is in you* [me], *than he that is in the world* (1 John 4:4). We need to learn to judge by the knowledge that God can make a way when there seems to be no way, as Elisha's servant learned when Elisha told him, *"Do not fear, for those who are with us are more than those who are with them."*

Think of Elisha's poor little servant saying something like, "Sir, I saw them with my own eyes. Come with me and count. I will show you. There is a great host of horses and chariots. One, two...how many thousands of them there must be!"

Then after Elisha prayed, he told his servant to look again. His servant was probably thinking, *I will look again, but I know what I saw.* But this time when he looked, he saw the mountain was full of horses and chariots of fire around Elisha. He must have said to Elisha, "Oh, there is a great God. Where did the enemy go? All I see now are angels all around!"

This happened because Elisha drew on God's wisdom and knowledge in the situation. God turned everything around and gave them a miracle because Elisha was moved by the wisdom and knowledge of God, not by what he could have first looked at in the natural realm. God wants to do the same types of things in our lives if we will just let Him. We let Him by understanding that He wants to empower us with the word of wisdom and the other gifts of the Spirit. We let Him by then opening ourselves up to receiving the word of wisdom and operating in the other gifts of the Spirit He has for us in different situations.

Think about what would happen if we believers focused on moving by the direction the Spirit gives us through the word of wisdom. What if we would make sure with every decision facing us that we have God's direction through His wisdom, through a word of wisdom, before moving ahead?

The Apostle Paul Moved by the Spirit of Wisdom

In the Old Testament times, before Jesus came, God moved *upon* people and gave them wisdom. Once Jesus came, for those of us who receive Him and invite Him to live inside us, God moves *in* us and gives us the Spirit of wisdom. New Testament events describe believers receiving wisdom from God from the Spirit living *inside* them, the Sprit of wisdom. In the New Testament, the book of Acts gives us many examples of the Spirit of wisdom giving the Apostle Paul information about the future.

Acts 27 describes the voyage by which Paul was being taken as a prisoner to Rome.

When conditions caused the sailing to become dangerous, Paul received information from the Spirit of wisdom inside him and spoke the warning. ...*Sirs, I perceive that this voyage will be with hurt and much damage, not only of the lading and ship, but also of our lives* (v. 10). The centurion in charge, rather than heeding Paul's warning, instead believed the opinion of the master and owner of the ship. The ship encountered a tempest, and after days of struggling to save the ship, the crew gave up hope. (vv. 11-20.) Paul spoke another word of wisdom.

But after long abstinence Paul stood forth in the midst of them, and said, Sirs, ye should have hearkened unto me, and not have loosed from Crete, and to have gained this harm and loss.

And now I exhort you to be of good cheer: for there shall be no loss of any man's life among you, but of the ship (vv. 21-22).

At another point the shipmen let down a lifeboat to flee the ship, and again Paul spoke a warning based on the word of wisdom he had received. *Paul said to the centurion and to the soldiers, Except these abide in the ship, ye cannot be saved* (v. 31). This time the centurion listened to Paul. He had learned that wisdom Paul had been speaking about the future was true. *Then the soldiers cut off the ropes of the boat, and let her fall off* (v. 32).

When the ship sailed into a place where two seas met, it ran aground and began breaking apart. The centurion gave a command for the prisoners not to be killed, as the soldiers thought should be done (operating in the word of wisdom had worked for Paul to *profit withal*—his life was spared), but for everyone on the ship either to swim to the shore or escape on boards or broken pieces of ship. The ship was lost, but everyone who had been shipwrecked reached the shore safely. (vv. 41-44.) Everything happened just as Paul had spoken by the Spirit of wisdom.

Paul had received a word of wisdom telling him what God was going to do in his future. Then he responded to that word of wisdom by acting on it. Everything in the crisis turned out all right, and Paul eventually made it to Rome, as he also knew he would from another word of wisdom God had given him telling him to fear not; he must be brought before Caesar. (v. 24.)

I believe that in these last days, God is going to use the Spirit of wisdom in a dramatic way like never before in the church in the people of God who obey Him.

Moved by the Spirit, not by the Flesh

The word of wisdom is one of the gifts that some people in the church who are out of balance have abused in such a manner, they have almost become cultic in it, almost like psychics or palm readers. Someone listening to the person who is speaking from the flesh rather by a word of wisdom may be led astray and say something like, "Bless God, I'm going to do what that person said because he is so spiritual. He told me all these different things." The gifts of the Spirit are not given for people to exploit and abuse to build themselves up in pride. God will not put up with such nonsense forever. He is going to raise up people to whom He will give the type of wisdom He gave Solomon. God will put a Spirit of wisdom in them because they will speak the words of wisdom the way He directs for the purpose of accomplishing His plans for the benefit of all.

There are many believers with the right motives who want to serve God and help other people, who want to operate in the gifts of the Spirit as God intends. In doing so, and in the excitement of being used by the Spirit, when giving a word we need to remember the verse that tells us not to add to nor take away from God's Word. This applies when speaking a word of wisdom, or when speaking while operating in any of the other gifts. When God gives us a word of wisdom to give to somebody else, He intends for us to deliver it without taking away from that word or adding to it. Some of us may add to that word because of what they think the person receiving it might need. Some of us may fall into pride, as I have pointed out before, to make ourselves look good and add to that word. The Spirit of wisdom is not given to us as something to play with. It is not given to us to abuse. God operates it through us to help people with their lives. When God gives us a particular word of wisdom to minister to somebody else, He gives it so that the person can profit, and He does not want us to take away from it or add anything to it.

Listening for God's Wisdom

As with the other gifts of the Spirit, we should operate the word of wisdom for our own lives. Doing this also helps keep us away from falling into the trap of abusing the gifts. If the word of wisdom is not good enough to use on ourselves, then why are we trying to use it on others? I try to live every word I preach. We all should live every word we tell others to live by.

The word of wisdom operates in my life. I make it a practice of receiving a word of wisdom for myself. I start seeking God early for His wisdom. The first thing I do in the morning, if I haven't already done it before I get up, is cry out to God by saying, "God, I need Your wisdom today. God, I need a word of wisdom."

Have you ever had the experience of talking to God, but He doesn't talk back? In fact, have you had the experience of it seeming as though every time you talk to God, He doesn't talk back? You ask Him for wisdom, and sometimes He doesn't say a word. You feel like saying, "God, would You turn up Your hearing aid, Sir? Where are You? Are you on the other side of planet Earth? I need to hear from You!" During those times, do you wonder, *Why doesn't He say something?*

This is what I do in these types of situations. I pick up my Bible and begin searching through it for verses or words I have underlined or shaded in. I search, keeping in mind the verses that say if I seek wisdom, I will find wisdom. I have yet to find a day when I have done this without finding a bit of wisdom to help me through that day.

There have been some days, however, when I jumped out of bed and rushed out of the house in a hurry without taking the time to seek for wisdom. I had cares of this world I had to handle. Because I hadn't taken the time to hear a revelation word from the Lord on those days, I went around all day long judging everything by what I saw with my eyes or by the way I felt or by what I knew or by some other way I reacted to the natural realm.

On those days nobody else seemed to see things the way I did, and what I found out about myself was that it was really easy for me to operate by a critical spirit.

Have you experienced something else along these lines when you realized that you had a wrong opinion about somebody else because you judged the person with your eyes? Everybody has done this at some time.

It is so important for us to seek wisdom so that through Jesus and like Jesus, we are moved by the Spirit of wisdom. We want to be like Jesus as described in Isaiah 11 who wouldn't judge by what He saw with His eyes; He would judge only by what the Spirit of wisdom instructed Him.

6

The Word of Knowledge

The second of the revelation gifts is the word of knowledge. We could say it is a "now" gift, a supernatural revelation of something in the present or something that has already happened, for our or others' profit. It reveals a piece of information from the present or past for use in the now that the person operating in the word of knowledge wouldn't have had the natural ability to know. This gift is one that people often mistake as prophecy. When they hear ministers or evangelists or pastors operating in the gifts of the Spirit, they often call "prophecy" what is simply a word of knowledge. The word of knowledge lets you know what God is saying and doing right now.

Let me emphasize again that the gifts God gives us are mighty. God does not want us believers walking around in the flesh and doing what everybody else is doing. He wants us to operate in life the supernatural way, a way that is above the things in the natural realm. He wants us to use the gifts, the keys to the kingdom, and bind up the things that need to be bound up and loose the things that need to be loosed. If somebody is handcuffed, the way the person will get loose is by having the keys to use.

People who sit in powerless churches just to keep their "fire insurance" paid up are usually as bound up with different negative things in their lives as are many people who live on the streets. Most of the time they are bound up and held by religious spirits. They are bound up with religion that is empty—those do's and don'ts that have nothing to do with allowing them to move by God's Spirit. They are walking in the flesh and many times they don't even know they are not walking in the Spirit.

Second Corinthians 10:3 tells us, *For though we walk in the flesh, we do not war after the flesh.* God's gifts are mighty and His weapons are supernatural and great for the pulling down of strong holds. *For the weapons of our warfare are not carnal, but mighty through God to the pulling down of strong holds* (2 Cor. 10:4).

Many church folks can't be what God wants them to be because they are held back by the many strong holds in their lives. Besides religious spirits, the strong holds can be habits, mindsets, or attitudes. Strong holds hold on to people and keep them from moving forward.

Have you ever tried to swim with someone holding on to you? I did this one time and learned it wasn't easy. I am a certified diver and love to go scuba diving. One time in Cancun, my wife and I were going to go snorkeling. With snorkeling, you put your face under the water and breathe through a tube that extends above the water. You get just far enough below the water to see how beautiful everything is there. For the lagoon where my wife and I were going to snorkel, there weren't any more snorkels and life jackets available. I told my wife, "You put your arm around me and I will swim." She had the snorkel; she just didn't have the life jacket. She doesn't swim—she would sink like a rock—but I thought this would work fine.

We went out with me paddling, doing great as long as my feet were able to touch the ground. But as soon as we were in water over my head and I had to depend on my swimming ability, she started squeezing tighter. The farther out we went, the tighter she squeezed. I started begging her to let off a little bit, to just hold my shoulders because I needed to breathe. Pretty soon, I was begging for some air, for her to release me a little bit, because she had a such a strong hold on me that, if it had been a little stronger, I wouldn't have been able to breathe or swim. This is like many people in the church today who are struggling and struggling simply because of the many strong holds on them. It's not that some of them don't know how to move in the gifts of the Spirit, but they have so many strong holds that they are struggling and gasping for a breath of fresh air instead of being able to move freely in the Spirit. Our weapons are *mighty through God to the pulling down of strong holds.* Our weapons of warfare are not carnal. They are spiritual, and they are mighty.

The next verse in Second Corinthians 10 tells us that we use our mighty weapons of warfare to pull down these strong holds by, *Casting down imaginations, and every high thing that exalteth itself against the knowledge of God, and bringing into captivity every thought to the obedience of Christ* (v. 5).

We need to be filled with the Holy Ghost, and we need to be seeking these gifts to operate in our life by casting down strong holds, wrong motives, and pride to walk according to the Spirit, not according to the flesh.

In this chapter, I am explaining the significance of why we need the word of knowledge operating in the church. Many times God uses me in the gift of knowledge and in the gift of prophecy when I am speaking at a revival in another pastor's church. On the first night, we may have a houseful of people when God begins to use me in the word of knowledge. It is amazing that at times on the second night, a huge number of people are no longer there. When I have asked the different pastors what happened, their answers have been that many of the people didn't come back the second night because they were afraid I was going to speak the word of knowledge over them and expose things in their lives they didn't want exposed!

But the truth of the matter, and the sad thing, is that the enemy came in and stole from them. The gifts of the Spirit are for our good. The word of knowledge lets us know where we are right now for our own good and what the enemy is doing in our life. Just as we saw previously, Elisha received the word of knowledge about the enemy, the king of Syria, to tell the king of Israel what the enemy was doing right then. Elisha warned the king of Israel by telling him not to send his army to a particular place. God had revealed to him the plan of the enemy to ambush the Israelites there.

It would be so good if believers could understand that, just as He did in Elisha's time, God is using the word of knowledge and the other gifts of the Spirit in the body of Christ today for the good of the body. We need the word of knowledge to operate in our churches today to let God reveal what the enemy is trying to do, or is doing, in our lives. This is one reason, as individuals, we need to be operating in the word of knowledge. I cannot recall the number of times that my life has actually been saved because of it! The enemy's plans were exposed.

Disaster Diverted

In one place where my family and I lived when I was pastoring a particular church, we had a cabin about three miles out of town. After the Sunday evening service, we used to go to the cabin. Because I didn't work on Monday, we stayed Sunday and Monday nights, then came back on Tuesday. One Sunday I had planned to meet a pastor from Shawnee, who wanted to buy a case of tapes, at three o'clock at the church.

As soon as I finished preaching on Sunday morning, the Spirit of the Lord spoke to me through the word of knowledge, "Go the cabin this afternoon." I was not very spiritually advanced in those days and argued with the Lord telling Him, "I'm not going until tonight." The Spirit of the Lord spoke to me again through the word of knowledge, saying, "Go to the cabin, and take your family right now."

I said, "Well, this just doesn't make any sense." I have realized since then, as have many of us I hope, that if we are going to operate in the supernatural, then the things in the natural things will not make sense many times. We have to learn along the way that whether we decide to be led by the Spirit or the flesh, the one we pick is the one from which we want to reap the harvest.

After the Lord spoke three times to me, "Go to the cabin with your family now," I finally decided that I should obey Him.

Let me tell you in case you haven't learned this, when the Holy Ghost speaks something three times to you, you had better do it! I told my wife and my family that we were going to the cabin right then. My wife told me, "I don't have things planned to go," but I said, "I don't care: We are going to the cabin now." I asked my associate to meet the pastor who was coming to buy tapes at three o'clock.

Later that afternoon when I went back to the church to hold the evening service, I saw police cars, the highway patrol, and a sheriff's department car there with emergency lights flashing. Because the chief of police, many of the policemen and people in the sheriff's department and highway patrol, and the district judge attended my church, I wasn't surprised to see the cars there, but I wondered, *Why do they have their flashing lights on?*

When I stepped out of my car, one of them told me, "Stay back; we are dealing with a situation. There is a guy in there who said God told him to kill two preachers in town and you were one of them."

I said, "What do you mean?"

He said, "The guy came here this afternoon with a gun and told your associate he was trying to find you."

When my associate had gone to the church to meet the pastor who was coming at three o'clock, the guy with the gun was there. He had brought a .38 cal. pistol which he had in his hand to use to kill me.

The story unfolded that he had ended up in a divorce, and because I had not preached against divorce the two times he had visited the church, he decided that I must be demonic. He said

God told him to kill me and the Church of Christ preacher. We were pastors of the two largest churches in town.

You see how that supernatural word saved my life. God gave it to me, but it was up to me to obey that knowledge. When God gives us a word simply by a word of knowledge or wisdom, it is up to us to obey that word. In the example in Second Kings 6, Israel was not defeated because the king acted on the voice of knowledge.

Many churches are destroyed or go through havoc simply because they don't adhere to the knowledge God gives them. The same thing happens in a family when God gives a word and the family disregards it. As individuals, it is our responsibility to obey the word from God we hear.

Set Free

Another example from my life shows how God can turn things around. I was ministering at a church in Kansas where my wife and I used to go quite a bit. This particular night the church was full. In fact, quite a few people were standing because there weren't any seats left. God was blessing people and moving—the glory of God was there. People were being slain in the Spirit, and God was moving in various kinds of miraculous ways. I looked toward the back, and the Lord said, "See that lady in the red hair, the real bright red hair." A saw the woman with the fiery red hair. The Lord said, "I want you to ask her if her heart is right with me, because I am not pleased with her."

My first thought was, *Lord, why do You want to mess up the good thing we have going here? I mean, we'll need to shut the music down and everything.* I tell you, the place was rocking!

I said to the young red-headed lady towards the back, "Young lady, do you care if I give you a word?" She agreed that I could. I said, "Come up here, if you would."

After she came up, I said, "Is your heart right with God? Is everything all right?" She said, "Yes, it is," just as simple as that.

I said, "You're living right, and everything is right with God?" She said, "Yes."

I said, "Well, that is not what God told me."

She said, "Well, it is."

I was thinking, *I have shut the music down. I have shut the whole thing down, and now I have made a spectacle out of myself. I told her these things God told me to say, and now everyone is looking at me as though I messed up.* Do you want to know what I did? I turned around and walked back on the stage to talk to God. I can see everything that happened as clearly now as it was back then.

I said, "God, You told me to tell her to come up here, that her heart wasn't right, and that You weren't pleased. And now I have shut everything down, the whole church has seen me and heard what I said, and now I look like a fool."

This was exactly how it went as I was talking. It looked as though I was talking to a wall, but I was really talking to God.

I said, "Now, what are we going to do?"

He said, "Go ask her some questions. Go ask her if her porch goes all the way across the front of her house and if it is gray."

The word of knowledge started flowing with more details, and I said to her, "Do you have a sidewalk that comes up off the street and goes right up to the porch? Do you take two steps up, and you're on the porch?"

"Yes."

I said, "Is the first room you walk into the living room, and then when you leave it you walk into the kitchen? Then you have a bathroom off there...," and continued until I had described every room in her house. This was simply by a word of knowledge in operation. I had never seen the woman or her house before. God gave me a word of knowledge for the purpose of helping her, not for the purpose of making me look good!

When some people in the church today want to operate in the gifts so that they can look good, or powerful, or spiritual, they are missing the point. The gifts are not operating in that context for them. They are operating to help someone else. That word of knowledge wasn't for me, it was for the redhead. It was to help somebody else who was in trouble. That word was given to me to bind and loose, to be a weapon of warfare against the enemy that was about to take her under. When I began to describe all the rooms in the young lady's house, she began to break down. She began to weep!

The word of knowledge continued operating through me. I said, "Now, sis, God says to tell you that he has not been satisfied with the traffic and with what has been going in and out of your house—in and out, in and out."

When I said that, she began to weep and cry, "God help me! God help me."

The Spirit of the Lord said to me, "Tell her now that I am putting a big angel on each side of the door, and I am putting a stop to that stuff that she didn't want in there but has been coming anyway. I am putting a big angel there, and I am going to stop what has been coming in and going out of her house, but she has to serve me."

Do you know what happened? God touched her in that time, and she turned her life around and was restored. How? By the word of knowledge operating for her good to expose the enemy in her life. We bound those things that were tormenting, those things that were destroying her home, and we loosed the Spirit of God on her house and in her life. She didn't go to a psychic or a palm reader. God used a bit of His knowledge being revealed to her that resulted in her being set free.

God wants the word of knowledge to work the same way in all of our lives. He wants to give revelation knowledge of what He is saying through a word on a daily basis. By revelation knowledge, I mean He will reveal to us a word of knowledge to help us.

Two Words of Knowledge

In Acts 10 we see another illustration of the word of knowledge. Verses 1-6:

There was a certain man in Caesarea called Cornelius, a centurion of the band called the Italian band,

A devout man, and one that feared God with all his house, which gave much alms to the people, and prayed to God alway.

He saw in a vision evidently about the ninth hour of the day an angel of God coming in to him, and saying unto him, Cornelius.

And when he looked upon him, he was afraid, and said, What is it, Lord? And he said unto him, Thy prayers and thy alms are come up for a memorial before God.

And now send men to Joppa, and call for one Simon, whose surname is Peter.

He lodgeth with one Simon a tanner, whose house is by the sea side: he shall tell thee what thou oughtest to do.

God told Cornelius that Peter would tell him what to do because God would give Peter a vision as well as a word of knowledge to expect three men (the three Cornelius sent) seeking him. (vv. 9-19.)

God gave Cornelius a word of knowledge. Cornelius did not know Peter. In this supernatural word, God named Peter and told Cornelius where to find him. This wasn't regular knowledge; this was supernatural knowledge. The Lord was showing Cornelius supernaturally what he should do and what would happen. Simply by speaking a word to him, the Lord told him who Peter was and where he lived, and once Cornelius obeyed the instructions the word of knowledge had given him, the Lord told him what would happen next through another word of knowledge to Peter.

In the same way, the Lord will tell us what to do. God will use the word of knowledge with us as he did with Cornelius and tell us where to go and who to see. Then when we obey and do what God tells us, He will give us additional direction.

We as the church need to be faithful where God has planted us so that we can be in place for God to give us a word of knowledge of what we ought to be doing. We need to understand that God wants to do many supernatural things in the world in which we live. He wants to do supernatural things through us, things that people cannot do in the natural, in order to reveal himself. For God to be able to reveal Himself by manifesting in our churches on a regular basis, we first need to reach the place of hearing God speaking to us as individuals. Until we begin to operate in the word of knowledge on an individual basis, more than likely we will never operate publicly.

Hosea 4:6 says this: *My people are destroyed for lack of knowledge....* In connection with this verse, we can understand why God wants to operate the gift of knowledge in us. He wants to give us a word of knowledge to tell us when, where, and how to operate in our lives so that we will know how to guard ourselves from being destroyed by the enemy.

I wonder how many church people have been destroyed simply because no one in their particular church body knew to hear or obey a word of knowledge that God wanted to give them. It is devastating to think about that. God wants us to understand that He is trying to reveal Himself to you and me.

Begin Operating in the Word of Knowledge

To begin operating in the word of knowledge on an individual basis, first of all we need to understand and recognize the voice of God. I called my sister's office recently and talked to her assistant. Joking around, I didn't identify myself when she said, "May I tell her who is calling?" I said, "I don't care a bit if you do." She said, "I know who this is—you're not fooling me." I said, "How do you know who this is you're talking to?" "Because," she said, "I have heard your voice enough to know it."

It is the same way with learning how to know the voice of God. We learn to know His voice by listening to Him, by being around Him, by talking to Him, by getting to know Him. When we get to know His voice, we learn to respond to His voice.

In beginning to operate in the word of knowledge, we start by listening to hear the voice of God ourselves. Some people in church say, "I'm waiting on the prophet to get here to give a word." Why do some of us think we need to wait for some other believer to come to town to speak for God to us? We need to know that God will speak to each of us just as much as He speaks to a prophet. God has to use prophets to speak so often because people don't know how to listen to Him individually. As New Testament believers in Jesus, we all have the ability to hear from God who lives inside us. In the Old Testament, God had to raise up prophets to deliver prophecy to the people to be sure the people heard His voice.

To begin operating in the word of knowledge on an individual basis, after we have learned to listen to the voice of God, we need to learn how to listen to what God is saying to us now. As we learn to hear His voice, however, we don't want to get off balance in the other direction and begin thinking the only way God will speak to us is directly to us. Besides understanding that God will give us a word of knowledge for ourselves, we also need to understand that God will give us a word of knowledge through somebody else. When people tell me they are not listening to anybody except God, they are discounting the way God works through the body to minister to the other members of the body. Wouldn't the disciples and followers of Jesus we read about in Acts 10 have been in mess if the only One they would have listened to was God speaking directly to them?

We need to be open to receiving the word of knowledge both ways: through other people, but first, through ourselves. People in the church often don't realize that many people will miss what God wants to do in their lives because they don't know His voice. People who don't know how to operate individually in the word of knowledge will miss what God is trying to say to them personally.

After we learn to listen to God's voice and to what He is saying to us right then and we have learned to receive the word of knowledge He gives us, we need to act on it and obey it. The word of knowledge is God revealing and unfolding His will to us. It is for us to act on and operate at the time we receive it.

In the word of knowledge God gave Cornelius that we read about in Acts 10:6, He told him, speaking of Peter, *he shall tell thee what thou oughtest to do.*

Verses 19-20 tell us, *While Peter thought on the vision, the Spirit said unto him, Behold, three men seek thee. Arise therefore, and get thee down, and go with them, doubting nothing: for I have sent them.*

God told Peter that He wanted him to listen to what the Spirit was saying to him—to go with the three men, doubting nothing. Isn't that good? God was telling Peter he could trust the men—He had sent them.

From the illustration above, the last point to follow as we learn to begin operating in the word of knowledge, is to learn that when the Lord speaks, not to doubt. Think of it as if you doubt, you do without! Walk in faith. That is when we are going to gain.

Verse 21:

Then Peter went down to the men which were sent unto him from Cornelius; and said, Behold, I am he whom ye seek: what is the cause wherefore ye are come?

In other words, Peter was saying, "Here I am." From that revelation knowledge God gave Peter, great things came from that—for the profit of all. When we as individuals begin listening to the voice of God and allowing Him to give us words of knowledge then we respond to those words, we will see that He is giving us this revelation to profit, as in the examples from the Bible. He gives us supernatural help for us to become overcomers and accomplish great things. God is good and He is trying to reveal Himself to us.

7

Discerning of Spirits

The third of the revelation gifts is discerning of spirits. This gift of the Spirit shows us the difference between truth and error, and it also helps us understand and recognize the spirits that are around us. We want to know, recognize, and acknowledge those spirits because we live in a spirit world.

Discerning of spirits, as with the other gifts, is given to us to profit for us to gain rather than lose. Many times we have been set back and messed up in our lives because we didn't realize there was an adversary out there. Many times we fall into the hands of the enemy because we don't even recognize that he is there. We can make bad business deals simply because we don't realize there is a devil out there tricking us.

I heard the statement on TV recently that America has never been in the confusion we've been experiencing during the last few years and at the point of needing to make the type of decisions that we have recently been facing. We are in a time when not only America has been in chaos and confusion but the whole world as well. America even in the Great Depression was never in the valley of decisions like America is in today. Joel 3:14, in describing the types of things on the earth that we will be dealing with in the last days, says there will be, *Multitudes, multitudes in the valley of decision: for the day of the LORD is near in the valley of decision.*

We are in a time today of decisions. God is not the author of confusion. (1 Cor. 14:33.) The devil is the author of confusion. In the time of decisions, the more confused the devil is able to make us, the harder it is for us to make rational decisions. As long as someone's mind is in confusion and chaos, more than likely, the person will make dumb mistakes.

This is what the devil wants the church to do: make dumb mistakes. He wants to cause confusion in the church. If the church is following after the principles of the world, and the devil causes confusion in the world, guess what? There will be confusion in the churches. One of the signs in the last days that the Bible describes is that the devil will try to wear out the saints. (See Daniel 7:20-25.) He is going to work to wear them down. Believers have already become worn out in churches. This happens often from becoming too busy in the way that Martha was as described in Luke 10. *But Martha was cumbered about much serving...* (v. 40).

Jesus said to Martha, *...thou art careful and troubled about many things* (v. 41). Martha's sister, Mary, was sitting at Jesus' feet, listening to Him (v. 39), and Jesus told Martha, *But one thing is needful: and Mary hath chosen that good part, which shall not be taken away from her* (v. 42). Jesus was saying that Mary was doing what she ought to have been doing, sitting at His feet and worshipping, but Martha was just busy.

The condition of many churches today is of just being busy. Churches like this have lost sight of the significance of what church is about. Attending church is not about coming to hear our musicians. Church is not about our song service or who is in the pulpit. Church is about glorifying the Father. It is about lifting up Jesus, magnifying Him and letting Him be the Lord of our lives. It is about sitting at the feet of Jesus.

We Need to Know the Will of God

God wants us to know Him. Here is the thing we need to know: the will of God. The gift of discernment helps us know the will of God.

In the final counseling session I have with a couple before they get married, I always ask a particular question: "Do you love her?" "Do you love him?" I tell them, "I want to know without a shadow of a doubt that you are in love, not lust." There is a difference. Both cause crazy feelings. Both the groom and the bride need to know it is the will of God for them to get married. Otherwise, six months down the road, one or both of them will say, "How did I mess up like this?"

This type of regret happens after making many other decisions without discerning properly, as well. Probably everyone has made these types of decisions at some point. After making a decision that looked good, felt good, six months down the road, I've said, "How did I do such a dumb thing?" I hadn't discerned what was actually going on around me. I wasn't discerning what was happening correctly and made a decision to do something that wasn't the will of God.

Making the Right Decisions

The gift of discernment supernaturally supersedes our natural understanding or recognition and lets us know the difference between truth and error. There is right and wrong in this world, and we have to choose between right and wrong every day. When we choose the right things, we will prosper, be blessed, and accomplish things. When we choose the wrong things, we will end up in deficit. When we make the wrong decisions, we will end up with problems—bad marriages, bad finances, bad jobs, bad environments, and on and on. Our lives are about decisions. Our lives are simply about the decisions we make. Operating in the gift of discernment in our lives is so important because it enables us to know the difference between truth and error in order to make the right decisions.

America needs to understand the simple message of learning how to make the right decisions through operating in the gift of discernment. From the White House right on down to our house, we live in a world of decisions needing to be made. The reason the times today are so chaotic is that we have not sought for discernment in the churches. If the church, meaning nation-wide, had been aware of and taught how to operate in the gift of discernment, we would have had more godly people who knew how to make the right decisions in every level of government. There are enough Christians, born-again people, in America to vote in godly people who know how to make the right decisions and to persuade people to vote for the decisions that will cause us to profit.

The problem begins in the churches not having enough discernment to know the difference between right and wrong decisions. We have people in the church who vote based on their party affiliation rather than looking at what a particular candidate believes. I am a registered republican now, but I used to be a registered democrat, and I vote for some democrats. I don't vote straight across the board for republicans. I look at each candidate. There are good republicans and democrats in office. There are some godly people who know how to make right decisions in office. There are some people in church, however, who always vote their party affiliation and vote for people who believe in abortion, for example. Doing that is a lack of discernment between right and wrong.

In our individual lives, in our churches, and in America there is an urgent need to learn how to operate in the gift of discernment in order to make right decisions.

How to Discern Spirits

Acts 16 gives us an illustration of Paul using the gift of discernment to overcome the powers of the devil. Paul was in Macedonia on a mission from God. Demons don't like the Gospel being preached. They don't like the truth being revealed.

Let the Peace of God Rule

Verses 16 and 17:

And it came to pass, as we went to prayer, a certain damsel possessed with a spirit of divination met us, which brought her masters much gain by soothsaying.

The same followed Paul and us, and cried, saying, These men are the servants of the most high God, which shew unto us the way of salvation.

One definition I read of a "soothsayer" is "a smooth predictor." Look at how smooth the damsel with the spirit of divination was. She was repeating a truth. This is the way the devil operates by giving a portion of truth.

Verse 18 begins:

And this did she many days. But Paul, being grieved....

She did this many days, then notice the words, "Paul, being grieved."

This is an answer to the question many people ask, "How do I tell if a demon is involved?" or "How do I know if something is the will of God?"

First of all, if we understand that the gift of discernment is given by God, how do we know when something happening is not of God? We feel grieved. Paul told us there is a way to know the will of God: *And let the peace of God rule in your hearts...*(Col. 3:15).

Let the peace of God rule our hearts. When something is not the will of God, it grieves us. In the Acts 16 illustration, the woman who started following Paul and the men with him preaching the Gospel began saying something to which, initially, they wouldn't object: "These are men of God preaching salvation." This was a very smooth method the devil used. Saying something that seemed to support Paul's work for God was the only way of sneaking that demonic spirit into the crowd where Paul and the others were preaching. Paul wouldn't have let her say anything if she had walked up and said, "I am a soothsayer, and I am here to cause a distraction and break things up"! He would have ushered her right out.

Similar things happen in the church world today, too. The demonic spirits don't come through the door in people and announce to the ushers, "Hey, we're soothsayers and devil worshippers; we're here to mess up the church." They operate as smoothly as did the spirit of divination in Acts 16.

The demonic spirits come in, sit on our pews, and act like Christians. Some churches let in more demons than others. Churches with wrong priorities that focus on having big numbers and drawing people in by various means above worshipping the Lord have quite a few demonic spirits sitting in their pews.

The demonic activity starts showing up in different ways to hinder the preaching of the Gospel. A church might start having division and then it splits. Then it splits again, then again. The people in that church say, "I just don't know what is happening to our church."

We let too many demons come into the church without noticing them until they become active. Some churches even put them in leadership by not placing godly requirements upon their leaders' lifestyles or the amount of discipline they have in their lives. It is something to note if the pastor requires someone interested in a leadership position to listen to a particular tape series, for example, and the person responds by saying, "I don't know why Pastor has me listen to those tapes before I get a position." If somebody is saying, "I don't need those tapes," that is a good indication of a demon right there. A rebellious spirit is rising up, a self-righteous, prideful spirit. I have had this type of thing happen, and I didn't even need to pray about it to know a demon was involved.

Paul took action to put an end to the demonic activity in the damsel with the spirit of divination. This is also an illustration of how simple it was to do it.

Verse 18:

And this did she many days. But Paul, being grieved, turned and said to the spirit, I command thee in the name of Jesus Christ to come out of her. And he came out the same hour.

Commanding the spirit to come out was simple for Paul because he was walking in the anointing of God.

A church doesn't need to have a demonstration every service of casting out devils in order to actually cast them out. In my case before every service, I go into my office and kneel at the altar I have there. I bow before the Lord and cast out evil spirits in the service before I ever walk into the sanctuary. I take authority over evil spirits manifesting. I also take authority over evil spirits when I walk into a bank, or any store— especially in a grocery store where people can run into you with those buggies! In other words, we don't have to make a big show of casting out demons or operating in any of the other gifts. One thing we do need to understand about demons is that they require attention, they require a show.

The spirit of divination was calling attention to itself. "Look! These are men of God. Look at me. Are you hearing me?" It was becoming louder and more noticeable than Paul and his men. This behavior is typical of the way demons act. Even though demons require a show, like Paul, we can use our authority in Jesus to stop the show.

I was preaching a revival in California several years ago when a man way in the back of the church at the night service started praying really loudly in tongues. After the second or third service of this happening, I asked the pastor, "What is going on with that man?" I know that some people have a naturally loud voice that carries; I myself have a loud voice, so I asked the pastor what was going on.

The pastor said, "Oh, he is one of our key men in our church. He is a prayer warrior." Instantly, I was grieved in my spirit. In fact, I had asked the pastor about the man because I was grieved. When that man had begun to pray, I became grieved and felt like I was all knotted up. I could tell He was not operating by the Spirit of God.

The next night after I had asked the pastor about the man, we were singing a song about the blood of Jesus. The service was about to be turned over to me. I was about to take the pulpit as we were singing, "Nothing but the blood washes away my sins."

I never will forget what happened next. I was sitting in the front pew, the first row near the altars that were in the front of the church. The man got up to draw attention to himself. He had not gotten any attention by praying really loudly, and when demons are given room, they will manifest. They are going to get some attention. The man came up to the front and started screaming louder than the music, "You people are my disciples, and I am Jesus Christ. You're my disciples!"

I had already bowed my head and was praying in the Holy Ghost, because I knew from the discerning of the Spirit that a demonic spirit was about to manifest right there in that service. I wasn't judging anybody—I just knew there was an evil spirit there.

After the man came up and started screaming, three deacons came immediately to try to grab him. What happened next was amazing to see.

The man took one of the deacons and slung him against the wall. He slung him hard. It was like the deacon was plastered to the wall for a second, he hit so hard. The man went after the other two deacons and slung them across the other wall. Then he picked up one of the altars and slung it like somebody would throw a javelin. He picked up the other altar and slung it the same way.

The church had been packed. The pastor had been excited because the church had never had those kinds of huge crowds before. But by the time the man had started throwing the altars, the audience had cleared out.

The demon had not been getting enough attention by simply mimicking tongues, and because it had been left there instead of being dealt with, it was going to manifest in one way or another. The pastor went up to the front and said, "In the name of Jesus, I command you to fall." The man wilted and fell to the ground.

The pastor asked me to come over and help cast out demons. He and I cast out about nine demons. I wasn't counting or naming them, I just knew there were approximately nine demons. Every time we started casting out the last one, a man would come in and say, "Let's take him to the mental hospital." The same man kept coming in and interrupting us, pushing us aside and interrupting our prayer. After thirty minutes of trying to cast the demon out of the man with the man coming and interrupting us, we finally did it. The next day, we found out both those guys were homosexuals.

Both men had been let in the church without dealing with the demons, which caused havoc and broke up the revival.

Breaking up a revival is exactly what the devil wants. He wants to break up a move of God. This example shows why the church needs to be careful to discern the demonic spirits within their local church to keep the spirits from interrupting, hindering, or dissolving a move of God there.

Doesn't Agree with the Ways of God

Paul gives us many examples of different ways he operated in the gift of discernment.

There was a silversmith who became very wealthy making silver shrines for a pagan goddess. Many other craftsmen made their living this way.

Acts 19:23-26:

About that time there occurred no small disturbance concerning the Way (NASB).

For a certain man named Demetrius, a silversmith, which made silver shrines for Diana, brought no small gain unto the craftsmen.

Whom he called together with the workmen of like occupation, and said, Sirs, ye know that by this craft we have our wealth.

Moreover ye see and hear, that not alone at Ephesus, but almost throughout all Asia, this Paul hath persuaded and turned away much people, saying that they be no gods, which are made with hands.

When Paul was preaching that the gods made with hands weren't real and turned many people away from worshipping them,

Demetrius was concerned because Paul's preaching was affecting his and the other craftsmen's business. Because the craftsmen were making shrines for the purpose of serving a goddess, it was obvious to Paul this was not of God. The demonic operation wasn't as subtle and smooth as in the case of the spirit of divination, and Paul immediately recognized it. In both cases, there was a demonic spirit operating to try to stop the preaching of the Gospel.

Another way of applying this account to today is that sometimes a pastor needs to point out things that are wrong, or wrong points of view, in his congregation. This is part of being in the office of pastor. The office of pastor is one of the five offices, or the five-fold ministry gifts.

Ephesians 4:11-13 describes five offices.

And he gave some, apostles; and some, prophets; and some, evangelists; and some, pastors and teachers;

For the perfecting of the saints, for the work of the ministry, for the edifying of the body of Christ:

Till we all come in the unity of the faith, and of the knowledge of the Son of God, unto a perfect man, unto the measure of the stature of the fulness of Christ.

When people in my church see how I operate in the gifts of the Spirit in revivals at other churches, some of them ask me, "Why don't you operate like that in our own church?" I do operate in the gifts of the Spirit in our own church, but I am operating in a different office in the revivals in other churches. The people in my church are seeing a difference between the office of pastor and the office of evangelist.

To explain, I operate in my church as pastor. I am a shepherd. I am to lead and oversee the flock. The flock matures in the things of God, brings other people to Christ, and ministers to people. It reproduces. My responsibility as pastor is to lead the flock into green pastures, where it can be safe and healthy, and to feed the flock. When the flock is safe and healthy, it reproduces, and this causes the church to grow.

Another of the five-fold ministry gifts is the office of the evangelist. An evangelist comes into a church and stirs up the gifts in the body and brings manifestations of the gifts. When I go into other churches, I fill the office of an evangelist and operate in the gifts the Spirit in that office. In my own church, the emphasis of my position and my purpose is different because I am operating in the office of a pastor, not an evangelist. The manifestations of the gifts operating in my church that I pastor happen in a different way than when they move mainly through me as I operate in another office in another church. In the church I pastor, the gifts will manifest in the services often through the members of the body in the congregation as well—the gift of tongues and inter-pretation, the working of miracles, and the other gifts.

The church I pastor isn't about me; it's about God, the Holy Ghost, and Jesus. Jesus said, *And I, if I be lifted up from the earth, will draw all men unto me* (John 12:32).

I am not the pastor in my church for a show. In fact, if I could be in my church without being seen, I would do that to just let the Holy Ghost manifest through the different members of the body. It's not about a show to see how many miracles happen when I, as the pastor, lay hands on people or operate in the other gifts of the

Spirit. Again, there are times when I do give prophecy, words of wisdom and words of knowledge, and there are times when I lay hands on people and miracles happen. But as pastor, I encourage the flock to focus on growing in the things of God in their personal lives and to apply the gifts of the Spirit to their daily living so that when they come to church they will flow in the gifts.

As with Paul pointing out the wrong direction people were taking, a pastor has an insight into his church that nobody else sees or has. A pastor is able to see what is wrong with many of the people in his church—things the people may not see in themselves. It isn't very popular to point these things out. But the pastor has to be able to discern those things in order to be able to help the people. A pastor loves his people, and he sees these things and wants to correct them out of love for them.

Sometimes I preach some things I don't want to preach. I say, "God, I don't want to hurt their feelings for no reason, but You know they will understand that I am discerning what is wrong with them for them to repent of it for their benefit, for their betterment." Sometimes I have a real battle within myself because I know that I am going to have to preach about something that I perceive is a problem or a need in the church even though I don't want to do it. But I know it is necessary because I am the pastor whose responsibility is to keep the flock safe and healthy.

An Obvious Demonic Spirit

Acts 13:6-10 tells us of a prudent man—in other words, a very wise, dignified man—who called for Paul and Barnabas because he wanted to hear about God.

And when they had gone through the isle unto Paphos, they found a certain sorcerer, a false prophet, a Jew whose name was Bar-Jesus: which was with the deputy of the country, Sergius Paulus, a prudent man; who called for Barnabas and Saul, and desired to hear the word of God. But Elymas the sorcerer (for so is his name by interpretation) withstood them, seeking to turn away the deputy from the faith.

Then Saul, (who is also called Paul,) filled with the Holy Ghost, set his eyes on him. And said, O full of all subtlilty and all mischief, thou child of the devil, thou enemy of all righteousness, wilt thou not cease to pervert the right ways of the Lord?

In this example we see a sorcerer, a false prophet, who very obviously has a demonic spirit, openly hindering the preaching of the Gospel by trying to stop Paul and Barnabas from telling someone about the faith. I have included these different examples of Paul operating in this gift of the Spirit to point out the different ways he discerned the demonic spirits. At times he was able to discern demonic activity because he was grieved. At other times, boom, he immediately recognized it.

The Gifts Come from the Spirit, not from Ourselves

The main point above all, however, is that Paul's action, as described in the example of Acts 13, was prefaced by saying, he was *filled with the Holy Ghost* (v. 9). These supernatural gifts come from and by the Holy Ghost. They come to us as revealed by the Spirit. These demonic spirits stir up trouble and demand attention. It's easy, if people are not careful in operating this particular gift of discernment, to allow operating in this gift to become a thing of pride. Especially when people see the power released if they then deal with the devils they discern in the authority of Jesus' name, it is easy, if they are not on guard against it, to become arrogant because of the power they see operating.

Some people who start out being used by God to help other people through operating in the gifts of the Sprit become accustomed to the gifts. They start noticing and really liking the recognition they receive and pride starts rising up. Operating in the gifts starts becoming a thing of pride to them. Some people can become so deceived by pride and thinking how important they are that they actually start prostituting the gifts for money.

We want to always guard against pride because Proverbs 16:18 tells us, *Pride goeth before destruction, and an haughty spirit before a fall.* Pride immediately precedes a fall. There were many great names—great prophets, evangelists, and ministries—that fell as a result. Pride is something all of us have a problem with at different times, and we all need to diligently guard against falling into it. First Corinthians 10:12 tells us, *Wherefore let him that thinketh he standeth take heed lest he fall.* It is important to refuse to fall into a spirit of pride.

In my life, I guard against pride. If a pastor calls to invite me to minister and says, "I want you to come and operate in the gifts of the Spirit," I turn him down. I start operating in the gifts of the Spirit even before I get out of bed, but I won't go minister to some congregation so I can exploit operating in the gifts or use them to show how powerful or anointed I am! I will not prostitute the

Gospel or the gifts with which God has supernaturally endowed me. And I will not prostitute the gifts in the local church either. I will not use the operation of the gifts anywhere in my life to show off. I prophesy, speak in tongues, interpret, discern, and use any other of the gifts when the Spirit moves me for the purpose of ministry.

When we mess up and make stupid mistakes, many times the reason is that we are being driven by a spirit from the devil that we don't even recognize. Many times if we aren't careful when Satan tries to come to us, we won't recognize what is happening. He will try to build us up in pride to get us to lean on our own understanding. Proverbs 3:5 tells us, *Trust in the LORD with all thine heart; and lean not unto thine own understanding.*

I experienced this myself. In 1986, I left a phenomenal ministry about fifty miles from my present church where I pastored about twenty percent of the people in my city. In four years, that church went from 40 to 800 people attending Sunday school. I made good money—a six figure income—and I was blessed. But a spirit came and talked in my ear and I listened. It said, "You know that the whole world needs to listen to you, not just this little town. The *whole world* needs to listen to you. And if you will go on television and accept the offer before you, you will go worldwide. You will see and do things you've never done before."

I let that spirit convince me that I needed to be on national television because the whole world needed to hear me, and I resigned from that church. God was getting ready to take me to the next level where I was, and I completely missed Him. The church had just finished building a motel and was preparing to build a convention center. But because I listened to that voice—took it in like Eve did—and conversed with that demonic spirit instead of dealing with it like Paul did, and let it convince me that, yes, I was somebody great who everybody needed to hear, I missed God and resigned from that church. Not only did I suffer because I missed God, but that church suffered. It went from the 800 it had grown to down to 50. When we get out of the will of God, everyone suffers.

To keep from making dumb mistakes like that one, we need to operate in the discerning of spirits so that we will not be enticed by those spirits and moved by them. When one of those lying spirits comes to try to get us to listen to it, we will recognize it and say, "Get out of here devil, in the name of Jesus, and shut your lying mouth!" Paul dealt with the spirits he discerned, and that is what we need to do.

I believe in angels and I know demons exist. Sometimes when I preach about demons when I am ministering in other churches, people come up and ask me a particular question. They ask, "Brother McGregor, now, do you think there is a demon behind every bush?"

I can tell some of the people asking this question probably don't understand how important it is to recognize that demons do exist and that God has given us the ability through the gift of discernment and through Jesus' authority to stop their destructive activity. I can tell other people are asking this question because, sadly, they have seen people who are out of balance abusing the use of the gift of discernment by spending all their time chasing demons.

These people abuse this gift by thinking God has empowered them to go around checking everybody else to see what is wrong with them. These people think they are operating in the gift of discernment, but actually, they are just judging people. They might as well substitute the word "suspicion" for "discerning" and change the name from "discerning of spirits" to "the gift of suspicion."

The gifts are not judging gifts; they are *ministry* gifts. Something that can happen is, if we are not careful, we will let our minds get off on thinking about demons most of the time and go around demon-chasing instead of keeping our thinking and focus on God. This happens when we start looking at the faults in everybody else but can't even see our own.

One summer, we had a demonic situation that came into my church during a revival. A man who had evil spirits in him, not someone who regularly attended our church, came in our door.

The man didn't want to be used by the devil but he was being used by the devil because he had no discernment in his life to tell him he was wrong or in error in any way. He told us what he thought was wrong with everybody else, and if we let him, he started telling us what was wrong with every preacher in every church in the area. He thought he knew what was wrong with everybody else but didn't have a clue as to what was wrong in his own life.

This turned into a very bad situation because the spirits in this man manifested in a big way to get attention, as spirits do. We had a visiting evangelist ministering who prayed for him. He and I dealt with the situation; however, the incident was so disruptive, that the crowds fell off (as they did when the man with the demon disrupted the other service I wrote about where I was ministering), and we had to close down the revival. The man actually tried to file a lawsuit against the evangelist and me, but as Romans 8:31 says, ...*If God be for us, who can be against us?*

All of us need to guard against pride, and we need to guard against starting to go in any direction when operating in any of the gifts that will take us off base. The gift of discerning of spirits is not for trying to discern what is wrong with everybody else but for discerning right and wrong in our own lives. It is one of the weapons that is not carnal but mighty through God to the pulling down of strong holds that God has given us to overcome the powers of the devil.

Do I think there is a demon behind every bush? No, it would be dumber than dirt to believe that, because the answer is: there is more than one. There are ten, eleven, or twelve of them behind every bush! Demons are cowards and don't move one at a time. Our priority, of course, is to keep our eyes on Jesus and on lifting Him up. But operating in the gift of discernment to recognize and deal with demons—especially in everyday living to keep them from leading us astray in making decisions—is very important to our success.

8

Faith

The three power gifts—faith, healing, and miracles—exert power, energy, that when released, do something. They are in us to use to accomplish things, to get things done. What does faith do? Faith is not just talk; faith is the substance of things hoped for. (Heb. 11:1.) It brings hope, produces hope, and produces the evidence in the natural realm of the things hoped for. Faith moves mountains. (Mark 11:23.)

Hebrews 11:6 says that without faith, it is impossible to please God. We need faith. We need faith to move mountains, to be healed, for manifestations from the spiritual realm to come into our lives.

Saving Faith and the Gift of Faith

In addition to saving faith there is a gift of faith. When we receive Jesus, God gives us a measure of faith to become saved. *...God hath dealt to every man the measure of faith* (Rom. 12:3). God gives us a measure of faith to believe that we are saved. When we are born again, we receive the Spirit of God. *Knowing this, our old man is crucified with him...*(Rom. 6:6). Our old man is crucified with Christ, and we have put on the new man. The new man has the Spirit of God. The Spirit of God inside us has the gifts to give us. The gift of faith is more than a spirit of faith, or the measure of faith, given us at salvation. It is faith to do something, to accomplish something supernaturally, beyond a natural man's ability.

All Christians are given the requirement to walk by faith. This is walking by the faith with which we were saved. The gift of faith is an extra ordinary faith we receive in order to do something: as when Jesus raised Lazarus from the dead. When Jesus said, ...*Have faith in God* (Mark 11:22), He was talking about the faith to move mountains. (Mark 11:23.) God gives us that special mountain-moving gift of faith to do the great and the miraculous, the kind of faith we see in the account of the three saints pictured on the Zurich coat of arms.

Men of Faith in the Bible

Daniel 6 tells us that a decree was passed prohibiting anyone from making a petition of any God or man other than King Darius for thirty days. Anyone who violated the petition would be cast into the den of lions. Daniel was not afraid to keep praying to God as he had done before the decree was passed. (v. 7.) Faith enables us to keep *doing* what is right. We know from reading James 2:20 that we can talk about our faith, but faith does things. Daniel was cast into the den with the lions but the next morning, ...no *manner of hurt was found upon him, because he believed in his God* (v. 23). This is a beyond-the-ordinary example of faith.

The Bible shows us that faith speaks. We read in First Samuel 17 of the giant Philistine warrior, Goliath, who challenged Israel to send out a man to fight him. (vv. 4,8.) David faced and killed Goliath, but before he did, he spoke his faith to Goliath and told him what he was going to do.

Verses 45-47:

Then said David to the Philistine, Thou comest to me with a sword, and with a spear, and with a shield: but I come to thee in the name of the LORD of hosts, the God of the armies of Israel, whom thou hast defied.

This day will the LORD deliver thee into mine hand; and I will smite thee, and take thine head from thee; and I will give the carcases of the host of the Philistines this day unto the fowls of the air, and to the wild beasts of the earth; that all the earth may know that there is a God in Israel.

And all this assembly shall know that the LORD saveth not with a sword and a spear: for the battle is the LORD's, and he will give you into our hands.

Many Bible verses direct us to speak our faith. Genesis begins by showing us that God created everything by His Word. Abraham, *...calleth those things which be not as though they were* (Rom. 4:17). When we speak God's Word, He watches over His Word to perform it. (Isa. 55:11.) *Death and life are in the power of the tongue* (Prov. 18:21). We overcome by the blood of the Lamb, and by the word of our testimony. (Rev. 12:11.) We need to claim the victory, and as Hebrews 10:23 tells us, hold fast the profession of our faith without wavering.

We can change our destiny by the words of our mouth. From Mark 11:23 we know that when we believe without doubting that those things which we said shall come to pass, we shall have whatsoever we say. According to Job 22:28, *Thou shalt also decree a thing, and it shall be established unto thee: and the light shall shine upon thy ways.* The Bible contains many references to making a decree. Another example is Ecclesiastes 11:1: *Cast thy bread upon the waters: for thou shalt find it after many days.* Proverbs 6:2 warns us, *Thou art snared with the words of thy mouth, thou art taken with the words of thy mouth.*

We are not to say what we are seeing with our naked eyes. We are to speak in line with God's Word. When we speak the profitable things, they will come to pass. Also, when we speak unprofitable things, those things will come to pass. The words we say will come to pass because Jesus Christ lives on the inside of us and our words are creative, creating our own surroundings. We want to pronounce blessings, not curses. Every time we speak, we need to practice choosing life.

Israel's journey through the wilderness was actually an eleven-day trip, but Israel wandered there for forty years. They wandered there because they talked about the past, compared their present to how things used to be, and murmured. They actually said things had been better for them when they had been slaves in Egypt: complaining instead of speaking faith and talking about the promises God had given them of how things would be in the future.

Many church folks stay in a similar wilderness. They barely get by because they talk about what they used to have or what their family used to be like. Many of them have a problem with speaking faith. They say, "Well, what if it doesn't come to pass?" They don't speak their faith because it isn't there. Romans 10:17 says, *So then faith cometh by hearing, and hearing by the word of God.* We need to stay in the Word and speak it, then keep speaking our faith.

Faith speaks. David spoke what he was going to do to Goliath, but he started speaking his faith even before that. He told King Saul about himself: *Thy servant slew both the lion and the bear: and this uncircumcised Philistine shall be as one of them, seeing he hath defied the armies of the living God* (1 Sam. 17:36). David was speaking his faith that the same God who helped him kill the lion and the bear, the same God who helped him do things before which had not seemed naturally possible, was going to deliver Goliath into his hands.

Before Peter got out of the boat to walk on the water to reach Jesus, he first spoke his faith. *Peter said to Him, "Lord, if it is You, command me to come to You on the water"* (Matt. 14:28 NASB). Then Jesus said, "Come." (v. 29). Peter came out of the boat and began walking on the water (before he turned his eyes on his natural surroundings and began to sink). (vv. 29-30.) First, before Peter ever put a leg out of the boat, he spoke his faith of what he was going to do. He spoke to the situation.

We need to start speaking faith to situations and acting on what we say. When we do, the supernatural power of God will begin to manifest in our lives. Sometimes we don't want to step out of the boat, but as we read before in Revelation 12:11, we overcome by the blood of the lamb and the word of our testimony.

In the Old Testament account, David overcame Goliath by the word of his testimony and by God backing up his faith. Speak faith in your life and let God back it up.

The devil will try to use circumstances that we see with our natural eyes to turn our focus from Jesus onto them. But we need to keep speaking our faith and looking at Jesus, and as Acts 17:28 admonishes us: live, move, and have our being in Him.

Instead of looking at the world's system, the economy, and talking about it, instead of talking about what the devil is doing, let's talk about what Jesus is doing in our lives. Let's talk about what He has promised us as believers. We need to say to God, "Help me to see it through Your eyes, not mine," and straighten up our mouths to speak in line with His Word. We need to keep looking at the unseen things of the Lord, because that is faith, believing in God. We need to believe in the unseen, and God will help us in every way He can if we will keep speaking in line with His Word. We need the supernatural anointing that will come to allow the Spirit to rise up in us and manifest.

To see miracles and healings operating in and through our lives, we need to speak that they will happen. We need to start talking about what we are going to have, sowing good seed with our words to grow a harvest to reap what we sow. We may not see the harvest for a while, but faith isn't about something we see; it's about something we act on.

I have a green house, and I planted tomatoes several months before winter began. By the time winter came, I had some very large tomatoes. When I planted the seeds, I used several large containers. Even though I planted all the seeds at the same time, some plants started coming up in only two of the pots. My wife said, "Why don't we do away with the other pots?" I said, "You leave them alone; I planted seed in all of them." A few days later she said, "My goodness, do you realize there are plants in all the other pots now, too?"

Just because we don't see a harvest coming up right away doesn't mean that a seed planted hasn't taken root and is growing. This is exactly how faith works. Most of the time, we have to wait for faith to produce the harvest. If we need a certain miracle in our life, we need to speak our faith over it and confess that it is coming to pass, planting the seed and watering it with the Word to produce a harvest. If we need something supernatural, bigger than our natural ability is able to do, we need to keep speaking our faith over it. Where the manifestation comes from doesn't matter. What does matter is that we trust God and believe that, *...he is a rewarder of them that diligently seek him* (Heb. 11:6).

When people say, "What if the manifestation doesn't come?" we can say, "What if it does?" When Peter got out of that boat, I imagine the other disciples in the boat were saying, "You're not only going to get wet if you get out of this boat; you're going to drown!" But Peter was saying, "What if I don't?" Peter would never have walked on water if he hadn't gotten out of the boat. Until we start confessing the Word of God over our situation and start confessing miracles, more than likely we won't see a manifestation.

In these last days, to receive the things that God wants us to have will take more than a measure of faith. Receiving them will take the gift of faith that is born out of His Spirit.

9

The Gifts of Healing

Mark 16:17-18 tells us that among the signs that will follow them that believe, in Jesus' name, believers will, ...*lay hands on the sick, and they shall recover.* Jesus died not only for our salvation but also for our healing. First Peter 2:24 tells us, *Who his own self bare our sins in his own body on the tree, that we, being dead to sins, should live unto righteousness: by whose stripes ye were healed.*

As with the other gifts of the Spirit, this gift, the second of the power gifts, is given to operate through all believers, not just through preachers and evangelists. When we become born again and filled with the Spirit of God, all nine of the gifts are available for us to use, and it is up to us to release them. Believers will lay their hands on the sick, and the sick shall recover.

As believers, if we see people who are sick, we should pray for them right there. Many times, instead, we think the right response is to tell them, "We'll be sure to pray for you at church." Why not pray for people right then?

When somebody is hungry, that person doesn't want people saying, "I will pray for you." The person wants them to fix something to eat. Somebody who is sick wants relief and wants healing. Some of us who don't want to pray for people are really saying that we're ashamed of proclaiming the Gospel. We have the greatest thing on earth, and for some reason, some of us want to keep it hidden. Others of us who do want to pray for people need to be careful not to want to make a show out of praying, either. We need to focus on walking in the Spirit and be ready and willing to release His gifts within us to help others.

When we make ourselves available as vessels, God will move. My wife and I and a man in my church prayed for his wife who had been sick in bed for five days. Her whole body was going into a kind of decay. She told me I was good at praying for headaches, and I prayed for a headache she had. It was gone in an hour or two. But then we prayed for her complete healing. I was standing at the foot of the bed and could see her foot, so I grabbed it and began to pray, "God, this is a full body treatment from head to toe." And God moved in with His healing power. The next morning, after being unable to get out of bed for five days, she got up and went to work. We made ourselves available as vessels, and God moved in a mighty way. I can't forget it. God wants to use all of us as His vessels to operate in His mighty gifts.

Healing Is not Based on Feelings

When this gift of the Spirit operates in someone, God's power flows through the person's body and drives off afflictions. When I pray for someone, I pray that the Lord's healing virtue will flow from the top of the person's head to the souls of the person's feet. Other people may say something else when ministering healing to someone, but when this powerful energy from

Almighty God flows, neither the person praying nor the person receiving may feel anything.

Healing is not based on whether we or the people we are praying for feel anything. Healing is based on the Word of God, and the Word says that by Jesus' stripes we were healed. If we were healed, then we are healed. This is a big area some people have problems with: standing in faith that they are healed even though they don't feel any different. We need to remember that healing is not based on our feelings. However, there are times when we do feel the healing power working.

Sometimes we may experience being prayed for and being obviously healed instantly—feeling and knowing we are healed. This happened to my wife who had been anemic for many, many years. Because of that condition, she had real problems with being susceptible to sicknesses. She even took shots and pills to help treat the condition.

One night when an evangelist was ministering in one of our services, he said, "Somebody's hands are really hot." Right before he made that statement, I had begun wondering if I had a fever because my hands had become hot, so hot in fact, they had turned red. The Spirit of God was rising up in me, and I had the responsibility to release the healing anointing.

The evangelist said, "Whoever it is, I want you to come forth and pray for people." My wife told me later that when he said that, I shot out of my seat like a bullet.

I started praying for people, and people were being obviously healed. After I finished praying for the group of people who had come up, my wife came up and said, "You've got to pray for me."

She had a need, and I had the healing in my hands; I had that gift operating in my life at that moment. She put her hands out in front of her, but I don't think we ever touched. At that instant, at that moment, power went through her body, and she received the manifested healing. She hasn't had to take a shot or pills for anemia since. She went up for her immune system to be healed, and it was done. Not only was her immune system healed, her eyesight also improved! Her eye doctor, in the two appointments she has had since the healing, commented that he could not get over how much her eyesight had improved. He was overwhelmed by the results of the most recent eye exam she took.

When we are prayed for and we receive healing in this way, we feel it and we know it. We don't have a problem believing for an instantaneous healing like my wife had. But the times we struggle with believing are the times when we are prayed for and the healing power comes into our body, but we don't feel any different. We may still feel pain or see symptoms in our body. At these times, we need to remember not to be moved by our feelings, but to keep standing on the Word that says we are healed.

It is one thing to receive a healing and another for us to keep a healing. I know some people who are prayed for and receive a healing then lose it. They go back for prayer and are prayed for over and over. Once we receive a healing, we need to keep believing for the healing to stay in our body. We receive healing by a supernatural act, and we need to guard and protect that healing. Something to consider is that after Jesus healed the man with the infirmity of thirty-eight years by the pool at Bethesda, Jesus said to him, *Behold, thou art made whole: sin no more, lest a worse thing come unto thee* (John 5:14). Isaiah 1:19 says, *If ye be willing and obedient, ye shall eat the good of the land* (Isa. 1:19).

We need to be on guard against something that can cause a healing to be lost—being in disobedience, in rebellion—opening a door for the enemy to come back in. Because the enemy knows he was whipped the time before, he will want to bring his demonic buddies to try to bring back worse whatever was wrong the first time. We also need to guard against being moved by our feelings if pain or symptoms try to come back. The devil is a liar, the father of lies (John 8:44), and wants to use symptoms to try to convince us we weren't healed in the first place.

Healings

Psalm 103:3 tells us that the Lord heals all our diseases. There are many types of sicknesses and diseases. The "gifts" of healing is plural because there is more than one type of healing.

Sickness and disease have many causes. People can become sick as a result of (1) an accident, (2) personal neglect, or (3) bodily abuse—people who abuse their bodies open the door for sickness. Another cause: (4) spirits of infirmity.

Many of us have known people who are sick with one thing after the other. Often the cause is a spirit of infirmity. As long as the devil can keep people inflicted and sick, they will not worship the Lord in the way they could worship Him. When people operate according to the way they feel and they don't feel like doing anything because of sickness, they won't do it. It is hard to pray for other people when feeling sick. The devil wants to use the spirit of infirmity to keep people sick so that they won't be effective.

Another cause of sickness is (5) satanic oppression. There is an oppression that actually causes sickness in a person's body. Medical science has shown that the bodies of people who stay oppressed and depressed release toxic poison into their own systems. Then there is (6) actual demonic possession. After casting out a spirit, Jesus told His disciples ...*This kind can come forth by nothing, but by prayer and fasting* (Mark 9:29).

Remember this: the only Scripture that works for us is Scripture that becomes a part of us. This is the reason we need to know the Bible and memorize Scripture verses. This is the reason we need to memorize verses on healing and prosperity and joy. The verses we know are the verses that will affect our lives. If we keep our Bibles on the coffee table in front of us or carry them around with us or don't learn any verses about healing or other areas, our Bibles will not affect our lives very much. Those verses will never affect us. But when we put those verses inside us, inside our spirit man, the devil will have a hard time trying to put us down.

I pastored one church for eight years, and for all eight years I preached faith, faith, faith. People asked me, "Don't you ever preach on anything other than faith?" but it's hard to preach the Bible without preaching on faith. I kept speaking scriptures on healing and faith into the people in that church; I kept putting that Word inside them. And in that length of time, with a congregation of several hundred people, we buried only two people. Why? When people have the Word on the inside, it is hard for the devil to conquer them. The two people we did bury were two who were very elderly and wanted to go on. When people get older than dirt, some of them just want to go on and be with Jesus!

Faith comes by hearing the Word, and we can read those healing scriptures aloud to build our faith and put them on the inside of us.

10

The Working of Miracles

For the working of miracles to operate through us, we must believe that Jesus is the miracle worker and that He is for us, working for us, and will work through us. When we confess Him as Lord, He is our Savior, our strength, and our joy. He's our overcoming ability. We must remember that our minds, our intellects, won't be able to understand how the miracles happen because miracles are supernatural.

When I bought my wife some flowers recently, they were just buds. She looked at them a few days later and said, "Oh, my goodness—all my roses are bloomed out." I don't know how they did it—I just know they did it. We don't understand how a flower blooms—it just does. In the same way, if we try to figure out how God does a miracle, we will figure and figure and figure. The working of miracles, the third of the power gifts, is a supernatural act of God.

I used to have a small-but-powerful magnet that could pick up nearly 300 pounds of metal. I bought it because I lost my keys on the bottom of a lake! I used to own some boat businesses and had a house boat on the lake. I had parked my boat in a little knoll, and the keys—a big key ring of keys—fell into the water. I couldn't get in the house boat or my businesses or my home, so I bought that magnet to retrieve my keys.

A number of people around there knew I had that magnet. When people had a similar experience, losing their keys or something like that, they knocked on my door and asked me to use the magnet to recover the lost keys or other items made from metal that had sunk in the lake. Normally metal doesn't float! Second Kings 6:1-7 tells us about a miracle when an axe head floated.

The prophets serving Elisha were cutting down trees with a borrowed axe. The axe head came off and sank in the river! One of them cried, ...*Alas, master! for it was borrowed* (v. 5). Elisha asked where the axe head had fallen in, then simply cut down a stick, threw it into the water at that spot, and the axe head floated to the top! The Bible said it swam. Then Elisha told the servant to pick it up. Picture how this happened. The man of God simply did what he felt inspired by God to do. In other words, he followed the unction. Elisha hadn't seen anybody else use that method to do something similar. It wasn't a ritual anyone practiced. He just felt an unction to respond to the problem that way. There is not a record of this happening before or since. Iron doesn't float or swim, but it did this time. God can cause anything, anywhere, anytime to happen by His power as He sees fit, and He gave Elisha and his servants a supernatural manifestation of His power—a miracle.

We see from the example of the axe head floating, a miracle that happened in an area other than healing. I experienced a miracle that happened to protect me a few years ago when I was on my way to the airport where I was taking flying lessons. I was leaving my office to ride my motorcycle the approximate sixteen miles to the airport. My secretary and my wife knew I was running late and in a hurry. One of them said, "You had better take all your angels!" I responded with, "I'm taking all 30,000 of them."

It was summertime when the oil can rise to the top of the road. As I was driving to the airport, I topped a hill where there is a crossroad. An older guy in a truck was starting to head across the road in front of me. When I saw he didn't see me, I didn't use the wisdom necessary to keep my brakes from locking up. With both my brakes locked up, my bike started sliding on the hot oil. I was so close to the truck—I can still see it today—I looked down and saw a grasshopper plastered on the front edge of his front chrome, and I had the distance of the rest of the truck to go in front of me. This was a big motorcycle but the driver never did see me or stop. He just shot on across that intersection.

I called on the name of the Lord and said, "Oh, Jesus!" I don't know what happened next at that point—if I went into a trance or something else—but all I knew was that when I came to my senses, I was 150 feet or more on the other side of the highway sitting there on my motorcycle in a gravel parking lot. I just sat there for a while wondering, *How did I get out of being in a wreck?*

When I recovered to the point that I could get off my bike and stand up, I started looking around, my mind trying to figure out what had happened. I thought that evidently I must have gone into a spin, and the truck's bumper hit my back tire and shot me across into the parking lot. I must have been so good at maintaining control of the bike, I surmised, I had guided it all the way over there! But when I looked, there wasn't a mark on my tire or anywhere else on my bike. I said, "Thank You, Jesus," and the Spirit of the Lord spoke plainly to me. This was one of the three times that the Lord has spoken to me. He said, "Son, you called my name and the angels took you over there."

There was no way in the natural realm I would have survived if I had collided with the truck. The power of God lifted me up and put me on the other side. There wasn't even a skid mark on the highway. This was a supernatural event more than a healing. I couldn't figure out with my mind what had happened because what had happened was a miracle.

I go about the day believing that wherever I go, wherever my feet tread, there is a need for miracles, and as a result, miracles happen around me. Supernatural things happen in my church and around me as a lifestyle. Although I experience miracles, such as the one protecting me when the truck crossed in front of my motorcycle, and see the ones the people in my church experience, I never cease to be in awe of them. I stay open to listening for the voice of God and being responsive to His unctions, like the one He gave Elisha to cause the axe head to float.

Many believers have not had miracles in their lives because they have been unwilling to step out and follow the unctions they receive from the Spirit. The Spirit will give us an idea that we ought to do something—we feel a little Holy Ghost urge. We might feel as though we are supposed to write a check to someone, for example, or say something to someone that turned out to be exactly what the person needed to hear.

I like to describe the way the gifts of the Spirit work through us as if we are a pipe for oil to flow through, similar to the

Alaskan oil pipeline. The Alaskan pipeline is a long, awesome structure. It was made strong in order to handle all the energy that flows through it. Many years old now, it is still a vessel for the oil.

The pipeline is not for Alaska. It is the vessel to move the oil from Alaska to the states below. God wants to equip us like that pipeline so that His power can flow through us. He wants us filled with His Spirit, strengthened by His Spirit, and open to His leading so that we can allow what He has for people to flow down through us to meet their needs.

11

Prophecy

Something that is "super" is extremely large. "Super" includes more than enough. God gave us the supernatural gifts of the Spirit for us to profit, accomplish, and succeed to the point of having more than enough. God gives us the means to succeed.

We have looked at some of the ways God has given us to spot and stop the devil's activity. Paul warns us to not be ignorant of Satan's devices lest he should get an advantage over us. (2 Cor. 2:11.) Paul also tells us, *But we all, with open face beholding as in a glass the glory of the Lord, are changed into the same image from glory to glory, even as by the Spirit of the Lord* (2 Cor. 3:18). God is moving us from glory to glory. And He does it by taking us through precept upon precept, line upon line. (Isa. 28:10.)

The first of the three vocal gifts is prophecy. First Corinthians 14:3 says, *But he that prophesieth speaketh unto men to edification, and exhortation, and comfort* (1 Cor. 14:3). Again, this gift comes out of our spirit, not from our head or intellect. First John 5:4 tells us, *For whatsoever is born of God overcometh the world: and this is the victory that overcometh the world, even our faith.* A prophecy is born of God and has to be birthed out of our spirit man then uttered. The prophecies from God are true. He does not make mistakes.

When we are operating in the gift of prophecy, we speak utterances from God to edify, exhort, and comfort the body of believers for their future benefit. God gives the utterances to build the future, not to condemn the past.

God uses prophecy as His number one way to speak to His people. Have you ever gone to church saying to yourself, "I need to hear from God"? Then in church a word of prophecy comes forth. God loves us and wants us to be built up, edified, and comforted. We need that gift of prophecy operating in the church for God to speak to us in this way.

Many times, a prophecy is a confirmation to let us know we are right on track. This is where comfort comes in. In my church, after I give people a word of prophecy, I usually ask, "Has God already said this to you? Does this bring confirmation to you of something He has already told you?" Prophecy should confirm or comfort.

For example, maybe a young man in my church has been praying about a situation, an area in which God has been dealing with him, of which I am unaware. He has been thinking and praying about this, struggling to know if the direction he thinks he should take is the will of God for him. Then in the service, a prophecy comes through me for him, an utterance confirming the direction God has already been giving him. The prophecy brings great comfort to him because it confirms by a supernatural utterance through another person the direction God has already been giving him. Do you see how prophecy works to really build up a person this way?

Seek the Spirit, not the Prophecy

The church needs a word from the Lord, not from ourselves. Prophecy can change the course of people's lives, and we must be sure to speak from our spirit, not move into the flesh and speak "prophecies" from our intellect which aren't true. Also, people need to seek God, not prophecies, for direction.

Some people like to overdo prophesying and get into the flesh. Then there are other people who like to chase after prophecy. Prophecy is from the Lord; it is not something we carry around in a briefcase to pull out and say, "Here it is."

I never will forget the night God used me in 1985 when I was in Nairobi, Kenya, preaching at the Full Gospel Businessmen's Fellowship International convention. The Lord moved upon me and used me very heavily in the gift of prophecy. I prophesied and prophesied and prophesied until I was ringing wet and could hardly move. After the service, the officials were taking me down the hall to the room where the speakers stayed between meetings.

Sometimes after I have preached a long time and ministered, when the anointing moves off me, I am not the most amiable or helpful person. This was one of those situations. As we were walking down the hall, a little black man started following us, then chased us down to talk to me. He said, "Reverend, you must prophesy to me. You must give me a word from God. You must give me a word." I was trying to move on, but he kept saying, "You must give me a word. Give me a word."

I felt like giving him some word off the top of my head, sort of like, "Here's word number 383 from my list." He was a little arrogant, and I could tell he wasn't going to let up. I'm not saying that what I did was from God, actually it was flesh, but I handed him my Bible and said, "Here is more than what you can handle probably." Again, we have people who love to prophesy, and then we have people who want to chase prophecy. Sometimes people chasing prophecy are looking for somebody to practically tell their fortune, rather than hearing from God themselves and drawing on prophecy for confirmation—for edification, exhortation, and comfort from God.

If people aren't careful, they can also start speaking from the flesh as if they are fortune-tellers. This becomes very dangerous. I cannot tell you how many lives I've seen or heard about, and I'm sure you probably know of some, too, that were thrown off course or otherwise messed up because somebody "prophesied" to them out of the flesh. When we are operating in the gift of prophecy and start to speak from our intellect rather than from the Spirit of God, we need to stop talking. Not to be offensive, but this is very important, and I need to be very plain: if it is not God, we need to shut up.

Test the Spirits

If we are the ones receiving the prophecy, we need to be cautious. If we don't understand a prophecy somebody gives us, we need to talk to someone like the pastor about it. We need to not run off and do crazy things because somebody prophesies something over us.

Sometimes people prophesying out of the flesh are easy to spot because they simply say dumb things. I heard a person stand up and prophesy one time: "'There is a person here who has female problems, and it's a woman,' saith God"!

At other times, we need to do as First John 4:1 tells us and test the spirits to determine if the prophecy is from God. *Beloved, believe not every spirit, but try the spirits whether they are of God: because many false prophets are gone out into the world.* If someone prophesies to us that we are supposed to marry a particular person, and I have heard people prophesy this way, or some other specific, this is a red flag. If we let prophecy guide our lives, this is where we go wrong. Remember that as long as a person speaks prophecy that stays within the scriptural guidelines of edification, exhortation, and comfort, we don't have to worry too much about it because we can receive something like that.

When somebody in a service stands up and starts prophesying, the person may or may not be giving an utterance from God. We need to be able to discern, to try the spirits, to determine whether the utterance is from God.

True Prophecy Builds Us Up

When someone genuinely prophesies to us, this is a very good thing, and it is important to be open to receive it. Our spirit is like a parachute. It works better when it is open! When listening to a gift of prophecy operating in the church, instead of receiving it, sometimes we will say, "That isn't what I wanted to hear," and reject it. A prophecy isn't necessarily always something we want to hear, but if we will receive it, it will build us up.

Not everything that builds us up is something we like. At my house, we make our own juice. I love the taste of the juice my wife makes with sweet fruit—oranges, apples, grapes, and strawberries. I will drink two glasses of it. But the veggie juice she makes with broccoli, cauliflower, cucumber, and parsley—my response is usually, "Yuk. I didn't order that." Then she says, "Oh, yes you did. You just don't remember ordering it. It's good for you. It does good things for you. I put a lot of green in it, and it will help clean you out!" To be healthy, occasionally we need to be cleaned out. Prophecy does this too. Sometimes it cleans out!

Office of the Prophet and the Gift of Prophecy

God used the Old Testament prophets to issue warnings to the Israelites who often fell into disobedience and idolatry. The messages often sounded negative, but actually God was calling the Israelites back to turn them around.

In the New Testament office of a prophet, one of the five-fold ministry gifts, the person will often, not always, but many times, speak correction. A prophet also speaks about something in the future and often about something specific. The gift of prophecy, as one of the nine gifts, is for the present edification of the church.

In this book we are discussing the gift of prophecy for us as Christians to use to minister to the body. We don't need to be in the office of a prophet for the gift of utterances to flow through us. We don't need to be standing in the office of a teacher, a pastor, an evangelist, a prophet, or an apostle to use any of the nine gifts of the Spirit in our lives. The nine gifts are not those of the five-fold ministry; they are the gifts of the body. We read in First Corinthians 12:14 and 21 (NASB) a description of the way the members of the body work together and need each other to function properly.

For the body is not one member, but many.

And the eye cannot say to the hand, "I have no need of you"; or again the head to the feet, "I have no need of you."

We as members of the body are to operate in the gifts of the Spirit as a lifestyle to, together, bring God's purposes to pass. We need to practice speaking a prophecy and operating in the other gifts of the Spirit. As we do, our confidence will build so that we will grow and allow the gifts to flow through us more.

12

Diverse Kinds of Tongues and
The Interpretation of Tongues

As I touched on previously, there is a difference between praying in tongues for one's own benefit and operating in the gift of diverse kinds of tongues to minister to the body. When we pray in tongues in our personal lives, we do not need an interpretation. When we operate in the gift of tongues, we deliver a message in tongues for the benefit of a body of believers, but because this message is not in English (or other native tongue), it requires an interpretation in order for the body to be ministered to by it.

Praying in Tongues in Our Daily Lives

Most of the time when I am awake, I am praying in tongues. People around me don't know it because I'm not doing it for them or for someone else to understand what I am saying. I don't even know what I am praying. Praying in tongues in our personal lives doesn't require an interpretation. When we pray in tongues, or in the Spirit, we are speaking to God. Our spirit is praying to God. John 4:23 says, *But the hour cometh, and now is, when the true worshippers shall worship the Father in spirit and in truth: for the Father seeketh such to worship him.*

Let's look at several verses which explain what is happening when we are speaking in tongues.

The Apostle Paul made the point that when we are praying in tongues we are not praying for men to understand.

First Corinthians 14:2-4:

For he that speaketh in an unknown tongue speaketh not unto men, but unto God: for no man understandeth him; howbeit in the spirit he speaketh mysteries.

He that speaketh in an unknown tongue edifieth himself; but he that prophesieth edifieth the church.

We are not speaking to men.

We are speaking to God (our spirit is speaking to God).

We don't understand what we are saying.

We are speaking mysteries.

We are edifying ourselves.

When I pray in the spirit, it is my spirit that is being edified. I used to have a John Deere tractor to clean up my home. Some of the best therapy there was for me was getting on that dozer. I loved riding along on that John Deere with that thing just humming and me praying in the Spirit. I just prayed and prayed and prayed.

What was I saying? I didn't know. What I was praying was coming up out of my spirit, and I was in tune with God. God was blessing me, and I wanted to practically live on that tractor.

Praying in the Spirit sure beats being depressed! It is hard for someone to stay depressed who is praying in the Holy Ghost. If I could put the benefits in a bottle and market them with a pharmacy, I would have a Number One seller to replace all the antidepressants being sold in America. This is what it's like when we pray in the Spirit and our spirit is edified.

When we are praying in the Spirit, we are communicating with God. We are blessing Him. We are speaking blessings to Him because we aren't using our carnal mind. Our spirit is praising God. We aren't begging and nagging God; we aren't trying to bargain with Him or trying to make deals with Him. We don't understand what we're saying and we don't need to because it is our spirit that is communicating.

Besides praying in the Spirit, the Apostle Paul also talked about singing in the Spirit.

First Corinthians 14:15:

What is it then? I will pray with the spirit, and I will pray with the understanding also: I will sing with the spirit, and I will sing with the understanding also.

We are able to not only speak in tongues but also to sing in tongues.

Jude 20 gives us another benefit of praying in tongues.

But ye, beloved, building up yourselves on your most holy faith, praying in the Holy Ghost.

We are building up ourselves on our most holy faith. Another translation gives additional insight into the meaning as, ...*[make progress, rise like an edifice higher and higher]* (AMP).

As we saw earlier, the Spirit makes intercession for us. There are those times when we think, *Somebody help me!*

Romans 8:26:

Likewise the Spirit also helpeth our infirmities [or *weakness,* NASB]: *for we know not what we should pray for as we ought: but the Spirit itself maketh intercession for us with groaning which cannot be uttered.*

When we don't know what to pray for or how to pray, we pray in tongues and the Spirit prays for us.

When I am teaching on tongues, people often raise a few of the same questions. Sometimes people want to know why we need to speak in tongues when we pray as opposed to always praying in English. Based on Jude 20, *But ye, beloved, building up yourselves on your most holy faith, praying in the Holy Ghost,* they also want to know why praying in English doesn't build up our spirit enough.

When we pray in English, the words we are saying come from our head so that we understand what we are saying. We are saying what we want to say. When we are praying in the Spirit, the Spirit is making an utterance through our spirit, and our mind is out of the picture. We don't know what we are saying. All we know is that out of our spirit we are giving an utterance. We have bypassed our head so that our spirit and God are conversing with one another.

If praying out of our intellect could always help us, we wouldn't need to pray in a way that only God can understand. Because our mind is carnal, our thinking tends to be imminent against

God's desires. When God tries to minister to us, we often react by arguing with our mind. We immediately try to figure everything out and say, "Well, I don't see how this could be right," then list all the reasons in the natural we think it isn't. Out of our intellect, we start arguing with God and try to dominate the conversation. We are also speaking words against the direction God is trying to take us, which isn't building up our faith. But when we are praying out of our spirit and don't understand the meaning of our words, we aren't dominating the conversation. We aren't trying to tell God how He has to do something when we are praying out of our spirit. He is able to move more easily on our behalf when we aren't fighting Him with our words and will!

Another advantage of praying in tongues is that the devil can't understand what we're saying. When we're praying out of our flesh and not speaking in line with the Word or with the plans God has for us, we are giving the devil an opportunity to try to use what we are saying to our disadvantage.

Some people wonder if tongues is like a foreign language. God did not send the Holy Ghost here for the purpose of giving us another language to speak. In the natural realm, no matter which country we grow up in, we learn the language spoken there to be able operate in that country. In some foreign countries, the people learn to speak three languages and use them in different ways. Speaking in tongues is not learning to speak in another language for the purpose of communicating in a natural way. It is a supernatural language that communicates only with God in a way we can't understand intellectually to help us do the supernatural things God wants us to do here on the earth.

Giving a Message in Tongues

Let's look at the group of verses in First Corinthians 14:12-15 describing giving a message in tongues, the gift of tongues, to the church.

Even so ye, forasmuch as ye are zealous of spiritual gifts, seek that ye may excel to the edifying of the church.

Wherefore let him that speaketh in an unknown tongue pray that he may interpret.

For if I pray in an unknown tongue, my spirit prayeth, but my understanding is unfruitful.

What is it then? I will pray with the spirit, and I will pray with the understanding also: I will sing with the spirit, and I will sing with the understanding also.

When we are operating in the gift of diverse kinds of tongues and deliver a message in tongues to the church, that message has similar characteristics to the tongues we speak in our personal lives: being understandable to God, but not to men, containing mysteries. We, and the people who hear the tongues, don't understand the words, the mysteries we are speaking. The message given through the gift of tongues is unfruitful unless there is an interpretation. God's purpose in the operation of the gift of tongues is to build up the church. It requires an interpretation for the people hearing it to benefit.

Giving an Interpretation

As with the other gifts of the Spirit, the gift of tongues and the gift of interpretation operate as the Spirit wills. *But all these worketh that one and the selfsame Spirit, dividing to every man sever-ally as he will* (1 Cor. 12:11). During the flow of a service, the Spirit will give different people unctions to flow in the gift of tongues and interpretation. God does not make assignments in advance by telling one person, "You give the message in tongues," and telling another person, "You give the interpretation after the message in tongues comes forth."

As I wrote before, sometimes the interpretation comes through the person giving the message in tongues. My wife is an example of this. Most of the time if she receives and gives a message in tongues, she interprets the message herself. Many people do this. Sometimes the interpretation will come through the most unlikely people, people we would least expect. At other times, two or three people may give different parts of the inter-pretation for the same message.

Sometimes people ask why a message in tongues that is very short at times has a very long interpretation. The answer to this is not spelled out anywhere, and my answer is, "I don't know." I have a few ideas why this may be, but the important point about this is to keep the purpose of tongues and interpretation in mind. The purpose is for the people hearing the interpretation to be built up. One thing we need to understand is that our Spirit will bear witness to the truth of the content of the message.

When a message in tongues given in another country is inter-preted in the language spoken there, that language might by nature express the meaning in fewer words than if a similar message were interpreted in English. Sometimes it seems as though English may take ten pages to say something another language might say in one line! Besides, I imagine the interpretation of a message in tongues doesn't match syllable for syllable. Again, the point is that God wants the content of the message to be interpreted for us to receive and benefit from the utterance He has given.

Steeped in Tradition

In 1977 when I was pastoring a denominational church before I understood the real meaning of being filled with the Spirit, I decided to attend a Kenneth Hagin meeting after my banker told me I should go.

At the time I didn't understand the scriptural basis for Brother Kenneth Hagin's teaching. I had even criticized and ostracized the Word of Faith movement because of my ignorance—I couldn't see that the movement was firmly based in fulfilling the Word of God. I was hungry for God, and when you're as hungry for God as I was, God can use that to bring the truth. When my banker told me that he wanted me to go to a Kenneth Hagin prayer meeting, I was so hungry for God, I was ready to eat just about anything that might begin satisfying that hunger. I invited a neighboring preacher of the same denomination, and we went to a Kenneth Hagin prayer conference in Tulsa, Oklahoma.

That night there were around 3,000 people attending that meeting. I was sitting there with a critical spirit ready to be judgmental about everything that happened. The first thing I began criticizing were the songs during praise and worship. I hadn't heard them before. They were verses from the Bible, many from The Psalms and Isaiah! I didn't even realize until later that The Psalms is a book of songs. I sat there with the attitude of, "Where did they get those songs? They're not in our song books," not realizing the songs were straight out of the Bible.

It seemed to me as though that part of the service went on for about four or five hours. It kept going on and on and on. Everybody kept singing, and singing, and singing. I thought, *This is the dumbest group of people I have ever heard. They keep singing that same song, that same verse, over and over, like they just can't get it.* I didn't realize they were singing the Word to worship the Lord and put that Word deep down inside them.

After the song service ended, Brother Hagin came up with his characteristic unhurried walk to the pulpit. I thought he was going to start speaking, but instead he said, "Well, let's all sing in the Spirit for a little while." I looked over at my buddy like, "Oh, man, now what's this going to be?" When the 3,000 people started singing in the Spirit, I had a reaction I didn't expect. I actually started getting goose bumps. I thought, *Oh, my goodness.* Then the hair on the back of my neck started standing up. I reached up to try to make it go back down. Then the hair on my arms started standing up. I began rubbing my arms to try to make that hair go back down, too. All through the auditorium, people were singing in the spirit, I had goose bumps all over, and my hair was standing on end while I kept trying to pat it back down in the midst of muttering, "This ain't God!" Then tears started rolling down my cheeks. I didn't realize that what was happening was I was being ministered to in my spirit. This wasn't something

I could understand with my head; it was bypassing my intellect and feeding my spirit. My spirit was being built up, and I wasn't use to that!

After that, Brother Hagin preached and had an altar call. Then he had people come up to be filled with the Holy Ghost. Following that, Brother Hagin said, "Before we leave, let's all pray in the Holy Ghost for a little while." That comment blew me away, what was left of me. I didn't understand until later that everything that had happened that night was firmly based in Scripture.

Here I was a preacher, through and through in a particular denomination, who believed that people weren't going to heaven if they didn't act like the people in our church. We had those really strict rules—you had to walk right and do things right; the women couldn't wear jewelry or makeup. (When people ask me today how I feel about women wearing makeup, I tell them, "Thank God for it—you can take any old barn and put some paint on it, and that will change the looks!")

Sitting in that Kenneth Hagin meeting, from my point of view, the only people in that room who were going to heaven were my buddy and me probably. I hadn't understood the things that had happened to me in that meeting, but I wasn't open to hearing from God yet. God had been trying to get my attention to show me the truth about being filled with the Holy Ghost and everything that means, but I wasn't listening.

Soon after I went to that meeting, some of the people in my church wanted me to go to Durant, Oklahoma, to hear a man whose name we are familiar with now, John Osteen. He was a Baptist who had received the infilling of the Spirit then was kicked out of his church. He was traveling around speaking and telling people about being filled with the Holy Ghost.

I went to the meeting in Durant. The place was filled. John Osteen was preaching a simple salvation message. Again, I was sitting there with my critical spirit in full operation, thinking, *My goodness, a kindergartner could beat him preaching.* I thought I knew so much more than the preacher. I thought I was so spiritual and had everything all together. I thought I knew what it meant to be filled with the Holy Ghost. I did all the things we were supposed to do in my church—I walked right, did everything right. I was so unreceptive and bored that I got up and walked to the back of the church to pray.

By then John Osteen started closing out the service with an altar call and asked people to come down front. As I was standing in the back, I looked over at the people who I had brought from my church. They were eating it all up—everything the preacher was saying they were just eating up. I thought, *You knot heads, I preach twice as good as this guy, and you're never this enthused!*

John Osteen said, "How many of you would like to be born again tonight?" About 150 people in the crowd boiled out of their seats and went up front. He asked them to give their heart to the Lord. He had them stand there in a line and repeat a brief prayer. A few people cried a little but were not very demonstrative. He made being born again that simple.

In my church, getting saved wasn't simple. When you went up to the altar, you kneeled. You cried. You balled and squalled. And you stayed there until you were "through." In my church, one saint would get on one side of you. That saint would say, "Hold on." Another saint would get on the other side of you. That saint would say, "Let loose." You didn't know if you were coming or going—whether to hold on or let loose. Then one of the saints on one side of you would start saying, "You got to get it like I do; you got to get it like I do." Here you're trying to think straight and give your heart to the Lord and you have these people saying all these things to you and pulling on you. No wonder it took so long to get saved in my church!

I was standing in the back of the meeting thinking about all these things and watching my church people eat all this up. I thought, *When I get my people back, am I ever going to straighten them out! They're falling for all this. They think you can get saved standing in a line like that.*

After Brother Osteen prayed with the ones who had gone up for salvation, he said, "How many of you here tonight would like to be filled with the baptism of the Holy Ghost and speak in tongues? If you do, come on up here."

People began pouring out of their seats to go up front. When the 150 who had gone up for salvation started to walk off, Brother Osteen said, "Don't you all want to be filled with the baptism of the Holy Ghost, too? Well, stay up here." My religious spirit really rose up in indignation then.

I said to myself, "They have not tarried; they have not paid the price. They are not even sanctified yet. They still have cigarettes in their pockets." Then I looked and saw my church people were going up front, too. When I saw that, I was really ticked off!

I said to myself, "Here I take these people to a John Osteen meeting and they go up to get filled with the Holy Ghost when they could have been filled at our church." The only thing was, at our church, the Holy Ghost didn't show up until after midnight. I said, "Here it is not even nine o'clock yet, and they think the Holy Ghost is here." When I was getting ready to be filled with the Holy Ghost after I was saved, I prayed and sought and bargained with God for a year. I thought everybody had to do that. But what it really meant was that it took me that long because of my ignorance in that area.

Eventually I opened myself up to receiving the truth from God, but before then in those Kenneth Hagin and John Osteen meetings, I was caught up in so much tradition that I couldn't see what was actually happening. I was putting stipulations on the Holy Ghost. I was limiting Him to when, where, and how He could fill the lives of those people. We who operate out of tradition for the sake of tradition and religious attitudes many times limit what God wants to do in our lives.

Seek the Gifts

If people are not moving in the gift of tongues and the gift of interpretation in a particular church body, the reason is not that God doesn't want the people there to operate in those gifts. Generally the reason is that the church has not sought those gifts. First Corinthians 12:31 tells us to *covet earnestly the best gifts.* Sometimes people don't want to seek those gifts because of fear. They are afraid of messing up and saying the wrong thing. We make mistakes in life. Messing up when learning how to operate in the gifts won't be the first mistake we've ever made, and it won't be the last, unless we quit.

Many times people have come up to me after the service and said, "Pastor, I don't know if I messed up or not because I had the interpretation inside me, in my spirit, of the message in tongues that was delivered in church, but I was afraid to give it." We need to realize that while we're sitting there in church, the enemy is talking to us. "More than likely you will give the wrong interpretation. You will mess up. You'll shut down the anointing for the rest of the service." And on and on. The truth is we have an advocate with the Father. God will forgive us, and we will move on.

After we seek the gift of tongues and the gift of interpretation, we operate in them by yielding to the unction from the Holy Ghost. The ability will not come from our intellect but from out of our spirit being. God moved upon Elisha and gave him an unction to cause the axe head to float. As New Testament believers, the unction we receive comes from the Holy Ghost inside us. First John 2:20 tells us, *But ye have an unction from the Holy One and ye know all things.* This means an unction from the Holy Ghost reveals all things we need to know; that is, all things we need to know are brought to our knowledge. Praying in tongues, singing in tongues, a message in tongues and interpretation are all given by an unction of the Spirit.

After we have made ourselves available to be used in the gifts of the Spirit and we receive an unction to speak a message in tongues, then we need to obey and give it. If we have an interpretation, we just need to be obedient, not let the devil talk us out of giving it, and yield to that unction. We may make mistakes along the way, but we always need to remember the result will benefit both us and the people to whom we are ministering.

Decently and in Order

As we yield to the unction of the Spirit in a church service, there is a certain way to do it to flow with the way the Spirit is moving. In a service, the Spirit is to flow freely as He wills and the people are to flow according to His leading, which will be in an orderly fashion. The Holy Ghost is very orderly and not disruptive. First Corinthians 14:40 tells us, *Let all things be done decently and in order.* Another verse that reflects God as a God of order is Ecclesiastes 3:1, *To every thing there is a season, and a time to every purpose under the heaven.*

If a service is chaotic, it is not flowing as the Spirit intends, and He will not be able to minister in the way He desires. Some of us have been in services where chaos ruled and know how disruptive it is. One person jumps up and starts prophesying while someone else in a different part of the congregation begins giving a message in tongues. There is no order in this type of service.

Some of us from my church attended a service held by a visiting minister where we saw a good example of maintaining order after a potentially disruptive incident occurred. A young man stood up and said, "Preacher, I need you to pray for me. Would you pray for me?" The young man caused an interruption, and as we saw before, demons require attention.

The minister knew the interruption was not of God. The young man was not following an unction of the Holy Ghost by screaming, "Hey, preacher, would you pray for me?" in the middle of a service. No doubt the man needed prayer, but that moment was not the right time. The minister handled the demonic outburst immediately and efficiently. He said, "Young man, sit down and shut up." Then he said, "I'm sick and tired of people thinking that this is a smorgasbord around here." He brought correction in that man's life. The minister knew he didn't have to pray for anybody at that moment. He would pray as the Holy Ghost gave him unction to pray. Some of us in that service might have thought the speaker was out of order, but he wasn't. He was bringing order to the church.

Had the minister yielded to that young man's request, he would have released the demonic spirit that was making a show by speaking out to take over the service. That initial outburst wouldn't have been the last time we had seen or heard from that spirit that night. It would have been in charge the rest of the service. Because the speaker took control and kept the service flowing in order, the rest of the service was in order and the Holy Ghost was able to continue to flow freely and minister.

When we have an unction to give a prophecy or a message in tongues, there is a way to give the utterance that keeps the service flowing in an orderly fashion. We will know in the Spirit when there is a place in the service for tongues and interpretation, and we should let the pastor or the other authority in charge know we have an utterance to give in order to receive permission to give it.

The way we do it in my church, for example, is for people to indicate they have an utterance by making eye contact with me or simply saying, "Pastor, I have a word," in a non-disruptive way. I will know 99.99 percent of the time whether the person does have a word from the Lord, and I will know whether that particular moment is the right time or not. People may definitely have a word, but sometimes I tell them to wait until I feel the timing is right. This way we continue to flow under the leadership of the Spirit in the service. If someone has a word from the Lord at a particular moment, the word will still be from the Lord twenty minutes from then. If I ask the person to wait, the Lord won't say, "He wouldn't let you give it, so I'm not going to let you say it."

Sometimes the gifts don't flow in a service. When that happens, we don't need to be all religious about it and think God didn't show up. Maybe there wasn't a need for the gifts that night. We need to keep our focus on Jesus and not become sidetracked with things that try to distract us.

Conclusion:
The Fullness of God

The Apostle Paul wanted Christians to understand our need for the fullness of God, for everything that God has for us. He wanted Christians to understand our need to be equipped with the power of God for our own lives and for ministry. But we also need to understand what the fullness of God means.

Some church folks think the life God has for us is to just barely get by, to have just enough to make it. Some church folks are interested in having just enough pews and just enough classrooms to get by but also talk about touching the community and the world. They have the right heart in wanting to affect the world, but to accomplish all they desire, they will need to line up their thinking with God's thinking of what living in His fullness means. They need to understand that God is El Shaddai, the Almighty God; He is the God who is more than enough!

In my church, this is how we think. We aren't concerned about having just enough. We want more than enough. We want to have more than enough classrooms for us to be able to raise up ministries. We want to have more than enough room for our ministries to be alive and active in effectively accomplishing things for God.

I decided and decreed that next year I want to give twice as much money to our church as I did last year. In order to do that, I will have to be blessed. Some people think we shouldn't make remarks like that. They are probably some of the people who think God wants us to have only enough to just barely get by. But it makes me angry and disgusted to be broke because God intends for us to live in abundance to do His work.

I heard a well-known preacher say, "If you're living on just enough, you are still in the wilderness." When the Israelites were wandering in the wilderness, God gave them just enough for each day. God wanted to lead them out of the wilderness into a land flowing with milk and honey! He isn't interested in us just barely getting by. He wants to bless us with His fullness—more than enough in every area.

Manifestation Comes from Taking Action

It is the manifestation of the Spirit that causes us to profit according to First Corinthians 12:7: *But the manifestation of the Spirit is given to every man to profit withal.* Having the gifts inside us or talking about them isn't what causes us to profit. The manifestation of the gifts causes us to profit. Manifestation comes from putting something into action.

We saw that "profit" means to accomplish, to get ahead, to live from the place of more than enough instead of just barely getting by. To profit from the gifts of the Spirit in our life, we need to allow them to manifest. We may be filled with the Spirit and have the gifts inside us available and ready for us to use, but to see the manifestation of God's glory through the gifts, we will, like Peter, need to step out of the boat. We will need to take action, to start doing something.

Faith is not just speaking the Word; it also is the action we take based on the Word. *So then faith cometh by hearing, and hearing by the word of God* (Rom.10:17). *But wilt thou know, O vain man, that faith without works is dead?* (James 2:20). Faith comes by hearing, but faith without works is dead. We need to speak the Word, but we also need to act on the Word. We may speak the Word and confess it, but if we don't act upon it, it becomes nothing. Faith requires action, and action—taking a step in faith—brings manifestation.

Some people say, "I need more power," or "I need more faith." But the power comes when we take a step in faith. God wants to equip the saints for the ministry, and He gives us the power we need to minister when we take that step of faith. We overcome by the blood of the Lamb *and* by the word of our testimony. Our testimony comes after we take action in faith.

To move in the fullness of God and operate from His strength, to move in the nine gifts of the Spirit, we need to be filled with His Spirit. To be filled with His Spirit, we first need to receive His Son as Savior and Lord.

Romans 10:9-10 states:

That if thou shalt confess with thy mouth the Lord Jesus, and shalt believe in thine heart that God hath raised him from the dead, thou shalt be saved.

For with the heart man believeth unto righteousness; and with the mouth confession is made unto salvation.

If you have not received Jesus as your Savior, ask Him to come into your heart by praying the following aloud.

Father,

Your Word says:

For all have sinned, and come short of the glory of God (Rom 3:23).

But God commendeth his love toward us, in that, while we were yet sinners, Christ died for us (Rom. 5:8).

...Christ died for our sins according to the scriptures (1 Cor. 15:3).

For by grace are ye saved through faith; and that not of yourselves: it is the gift of God (Eph. 2:8).

I confess with my mouth that Jesus is Lord and believe in my heart that You raised Him from the dead. I receive Jesus as my Savior and Lord as a gift from You. Thank You for sending Him to die for my sins.

In Jesus' name, amen.

Be Filled with the Spirit

John baptized with water but Jesus baptized with the Holy Ghost and fire.

Acts 1:5 tells us, *For John truly baptized with water; but ye shall be baptized with the Holy Ghost not many days hence.*

John said, *I indeed baptize you with water unto repentance: but he that cometh after me is mightier than I, whose shoes I am not worthy to bear: he shall baptize you with the Holy Ghost, and with fire* (Matt. 3:11).

Acts 1:8 says, *But ye shall receive power, after that the Holy Ghost is come upon you: and ye shall be witnesses unto me both in Jerusalem, and in all Judaea, and in Samaria, and unto the uttermost part of the earth.*

If you would like Jesus to baptize you with the Holy Spirit and receive power to witness and live a life of victory in God, pray the following.

Father,

Your Word says,

If ye then, being evil, know how to give good gifts unto your children: how much more shall your heavenly Father give the Holy Spirit to them that ask him? (Luke 11:13).

And they were all filled with the Holy Ghost, and began to speak with other tongues, as the Spirit gave them utterance (Acts 2:4).

I want to be filled to overflowing with Your Spirit and operate in the fullness of Your power, and I ask You to baptize me with Your Spirit. I believe I receive the infilling of Your Holy Spirit with the evidence of speaking in tongues operating through me. Thank You. In Jesus' name, I pray. Amen.

Once you have received, you have the ability to speak in tongues as the Spirit gives you utterance. Yield yourself to the Spirit; yield your tongue to speaking syllables that you don't understand. You may speak only a few syllables at first, or you may begin speaking easily in tongues. You have the ability to start and stop. Begin praying in the Spirit regularly to build yourself up on your Holy Faith.

You now have the power of the Holy Spirit available to you to minister through the nine gifts of the Spirit. Balance moving in the gifts with developing the fruit of the Spirit and step out in faith motivated by charity, love in action, to burn bright with the Light of Jesus.

CPSIA information can be obtained at www.ICGtesting.com
Printed in the USA
LVOW031003031111

253323LV00003B/5/P